No Nonsense English

10–11 years

Central pull-out pages

Parents' notes   A1
Answers   A2–4

Contents

Lesson		Pages
	Handwriting practice	2–3
1–6	Spelling	4–9
	Unstressed vowels • Word roots • Suffixes • Connectives • Homophones 1 • 'ough' words	
7–11	Grammar	10–14
	Prepositions • Conventions • Complex sentences • Active and passive 1 • Active and passive 2	
12–14	Punctuation	15–17
	Colons and semicolons • Hyphens and dashes • Commas and brackets	
15–16	Comprehension	18–21
	Classic fiction • Non-chronological reports	
	How am I doing?	22–23
17–22	Spelling	24–29
	Unstressed letters • Prefixes • Spelling strategies 1 • Spelling strategies 2 • Homophones 2 • Homophones 3 • Making adjectives	
23–27	Grammar	30–34
	Active and passive 3 • Formal language • Complex sentences • Clauses 1 • Clauses 2	
28–30	Punctuation	35–37
	Apostrophes • Dialogue • Commas	
31–32	Comprehension	38–41
	Nonsense poetry • Balanced arguments	
	How am I doing?	42–43
33–38	Spelling	44–49
	Spelling rules 1 • Spelling rules 2 • Spelling rules 3 • Irregular words • Similes • Metaphors	
39–43	Grammar	50–54
	Modal verbs • Instructional texts 1 • Persuasive texts • Impersonal writing • Synonyms and antonyms	
44–46	Punctuation	55–57
	Forms of punctuation • Bullet points • Instructional texts 2	
47–48	Comprehension	58–61
	Comparing poems • Skimming and scanning	
	How am I doing?	62–63

Handwriting practice

Copy this poem on the lines underneath.

The Pobble who has no toes

The Pobble who has no toes
Had once as many as we;
When they said "Some day you may lose them all;"
He replied "Fish, fiddle-de-dee!"
And his Aunt Jobiska made him drink
Lavender water tinged with pink,
For she said "The World in general knows
There's nothing so good for a Pobble's toes!"

Copy this piece of writing on the lines underneath.

Treasure Island

I remember him as if it were yesterday. He came plodding to the inn door – a tall, strong, heavy, nut-brown man, his tarry pigtail falling over the shoulder of his soiled blue coat, his hands ragged and scarred, with black, broken nails, and the sabre cut across one cheek. I remember him breaking out in that old sea-song that he sang so often afterwards: "Fifteen men on the dead man's chest – Yo-ho-ho, and a bottle of rum!"

Lesson 1 | Spelling

Unstressed vowels

> **Unstressed vowels** are either:
> • not sounded clearly, for example the second 'a' in par**a**llel (it sounds like 'uh')
> OR
> • not sounded at all, for example the 'e' in g**e**ography.

QUICK TIP! Use a dictionary to look up any spellings you are unsure about.

1. Say these words and underline the unstressed vowels.

   a fattening   b dandelion   c miniature   d interest   e astronomy
   f abandon   g lettuce   h benefit   i journalist j mathematics

2. Write the unstressed vowels in these words.

   a tel_vision   b parli__ment   c veg_table   d cons_n_nt   e cemet_ry
   f ov_n   g sign_ture   h med_cine   i muscl_   j gramm_r

3. These words have unstressed vowels in them. Underline the words that are spelt correctly.

   a separate seperate   b definate definite   c intresting interesting
   d teluphone telephone   e nuisance nusance   f secrutry secretary
   g mischevus mischievous   h temperature temprature   i lemonade lemunade

4. When a word ending in ary, ery or ory is spoken it can be hard to tell how to spell the ending. Write the words in the correct columns depending upon their endings.

   (6 marks)

Words	ary endings	ery endings	ory endings
lott _ _ _ Febru _ _ _			
hist _ _ _ Janu _ _ _			
fact _ _ _ bound _ _ _			
categ _ _ _ station _ _ _			
volunt _ _ _ jewell _ _ _			
batt _ _ _ veterin _ _ _			

QUICK TIP! One word belongs in two columns. Which word is it?

0			35
Tough		OK	Got it!

Total  /35

Word roots

Spelling — Lesson 2

Many words, such as **pay** or **day**, can be used as root words. Prefixes or suffixes can be added to a root word to create a new word:

repay   **payment**

Sometimes the new words will be compound words:

daylight   **birthday**

1. **Find the root word hidden inside the longer word. The first one has been done for you.**

   a indigestible   concept   b decipherable   learn
   c preferential   correspond   d hyphenated   integrate
   e correspondent   digest   f disintegration   cipher
   g misconception   prefer   h unlearned   hyphen

2. **Write three new words using each root word.**

   a fire   _____   _____   _____
   b commit   _____   _____   _____
   c special   _____   _____   _____
   d fort   _____   _____   _____
   e safe   _____   _____   _____

3. **Complete these definitions by adding prefixes to the given words and groups of letters.**

   inter   post   pre   sub   super   trans   contra

   a To sink or plunge under the water = _____merge
   b An addition to the end of a letter = _____script
   c To change the form, character or appearance of something = _____form
   d Something that is unnecessary, extra to one's needs = _____fluous
   e To break in when someone is speaking = _____rupt
   f To argue an opposing point of view = _____dict
   g To get ready for something = _____pare

| 0 | Tough | OK | Got it! | 19 |

Total /19

Lesson 3 | Spelling

Suffixes

A suffix is added to the end of a word to make a new but related word.
laugh   laughable
If a word ends with **e** delete the **e** and add the suffix.
office   official
If a word ends in **r** double the **r** and add the ending.
refer   referring   reference

1. Select the correct suffixes: -ant, -ance, -ment, -al

   a command _____   _____

   b ignore _____   _____

   c inform _____   _____

   d attend _____   _____

2. Add the suffix ial to these words.

   a substance _____   b commerce _____   c part _____

   d finance _____   e confident _____   f artifice _____

   g race _____   h province _____   i deny _____

3. Add able or ible to these words.

   a adore _____   b notice _____   c enjoy _____

   d sense _____   e change _____   f force _____

4. Add suffixes to make other forms of these verbs.

   a prefer _____   _____

   b music   _____   _____

   c break   _____   _____

| 0 | Tough | OK | Got it! | 22 |

Total /22

Connectives

Spelling | Lesson 4

> **Connectives** connect clauses and sentences together. When two clauses are joined you get two thoughts or actions in the same sentence. Connectives can be:
> - short words, like **if**
> - made up of two or more words, like **notwithstanding**
> - phrases, like **because of**.

1. Underline the connectives in these sentences.

   a We had our tea then we played football.

   b We did some practice after we tuned our guitars.

   c I'd had enough so I went home.

   d Coach was cross because I missed a free kick.

2. Match pairs of words together to make connectives and write them on the line.

   a where   ever   _____

   b how   while   _____

   c there   ever   _____

   d what   over   _____

   e who   fore   _____

   f mean   ever   _____

   g more   as   _____

3. Join three words together to make two compound connectives.

   never   so   far   a _____

   in   the   less   b _____

4. Group these connectives according to type.

   secondly meanwhile therefore lastly so afterwards

time	sequence	logic

   (6 marks)

	Tough	OK	Got it!	
0				19

Total /19

Lesson 5 | Spelling

Homophones 1

> The word **homophone** is made from two words:
>
> **homo** means **same**   **phone** means **sound**
>
> Homophones are words that sound the same but are spelt differently and have different meanings: **no** and **know** – It was no good. I didn't know that!

1. **Link the homophones that sound the same**

   a aisle   alter   b aloud   assent

   c bawl   isle   d ascent   bridle

   e altar   ball   f bridal   allowed

2. **Fill in the gaps with the correct homophones.**

   principles/principals, heard/herd, further/father, guest/guessed

   a The _____ of both colleges had strong basic _____.

   b In the distance they _____ a _____ of elephants.

   c He asked his _____ how much _____ it was.

   d She _____ their _____ would arrive on time.

3. **Fill in the correct homophones.**

   who's, whose, passed, past, led, lead, dessert, desert

   a Mum, _____ coming to tea?   b _____ bike is that?

   c He _____ the way home.   d The box was as heavy as _____.

   e She _____ the ball to me.   f It was all in the _____.

   g They crossed the sandy _____.   h They had ice cream for _____.

0			18
Tough	OK	Got it!	

Total

'ough' words

Spelling — Lesson 6

> 'ough' words have several pronunciations. Here are some of them: **aw, off, uff, oh, oo, ow**.

1. What are the pronunciations of these words?

    a rough _____   b ought _____   c through _____

    d though _____   e plough _____   f cough _____

2. Use the words above to complete these sentences.

    a They ran _____ the woods.

    b Terry had a bad _____.

    c I _____ to leave now as it's getting late.

    d Even _____ it was cold they went out to play.

    e After harvesting, farmers _____ their fields.

    f The sea was very _____ so the boat tossed and turned.

3. Use these words to complete these sentences: though, through, thorough.

    a She made a _____ search for her badge.

    b She went _____ all her pockets and bags.

    c Even _____ it was late she went on looking.

    d Her _____ search was successful and she found her badge.

0			16	Total
Tough	OK	Got it!		/16

Lesson 7 | Grammar

Prepositions

> **Prepositions** are words or phrases used before a noun or pronoun to link it to another part of the sentence. They often indicate:
> - **direction** (**over** the hill, **up** the stairs)
> - **position** (**in** a car, **behind** the door)
> - **time** (**during** the film, **on** Monday)

1. **Choose a preposition to complete each sentence. Use each preposition once.**

   during   off   behind   on   through   under   up   across   in   around

   a Calvin jumped _____ the diving board.

   b They ran _____ the road.

   c Susan looked _____ the window.

   d They chased each other _____ the playground.

   e The squirrel scrambled _____ the tree.

   f There was a terrific thunderstorm _____ the night.

   g Rosie crawled _____ her bed looking for her shoe.

   h He crept up _____ his dad and poked him _____ the ribs.

   i The notice went up _____ the notice board yesterday morning.

   QUICK TIP!
   Write in pencil so that you can rub a word out if you need to!

2. **Select one of the prepositional phrases to complete these sentences.**

   by means of   in accordance with   in spite of   because of

   a She came with us _____ all she had said.

   b We got there eventually _____ public transport.

   c We set up the experiment _____ the instructions.

   d The pavements were icy _____ the steep drop in temperature.

Conventions

Grammar | **Lesson 8**

> In all languages there are rules about the order of words in a sentence, just as there are rules about the letters in a word. There also has to be agreement between the articles, nouns, pronouns, adjectives, verbs and adverbs.

1. **Choose the correct article for these phrases: a, an, some.**

   a _____ trolley   b _____ orange   c _____ pears   d _____ basket
   e _____ new shoes   f _____ object   g _____ apple   h _____ road

2. **Rearrange and rewrite these phrases so that the adjectives and nouns agree with each other.**

   a some bike yellow _____   b those six pencil _____

   c a nice houses _____   d an cases empty _____

   e my own beds _____   f the day old good _____

3. **Change the tense of these verbs to agree with the adverbs.**

   a Ivan saw her tomorrow. _____

   b I will go yesterday. _____

   c Len ran next Sunday. _____

   d Mary will dance last Saturday. _____

   e Ivan played on his Gameboy tomorrow. _____

4. **Rewrite these sentences so that the verb tense and the nouns agree with the rest of the sentence.**

   a It is fun to went on holiday. _____

   b I like played in the park. _____

   c Bob stays in beds late this morning. _____

   d Tom will trip over a stones yesterday morning. _____

   e Lena will swim several races last Wednesday. _____

   f A leopard cannot changed his spot. _____

   g You must be homes before sevens o'clock. _____

   h The early bird catched the worms. _____

0	Tough	OK	Got it! 27

Total: 27

Lesson 9 | Grammar

Complex sentences

> A complex sentence has a **main clause** and a **subordinate clause**.
> A **main clause** makes sense on its own.
> A **subordinate clause** does not make sense on its own.
>   When it started to snow, I went indoors.
>   subordinate clause   main clause
> The subordinate clause adds information to the main clause and starts with a conjunction such as **since**, **when**, **while**, **although**.

1. **Underline the main clauses in these sentences and circle the subordinate clauses.**

    a If we hurry, we will catch the next bus.

    b When the bell rang, we went out into the playground.

    c He turned off the lights, before he went out.

    d To keep the Mongols out of China, the Emperor built the Great Wall.

2. **Choose a connective to complete these complex sentences.**

    after   when   in case   until   since   because   even though   although

    a _____ it was time to go, Susie put her coat on.

    b Paul listened to some music _____ she had gone.

    c He was enjoying it _____ his mum yelled at him.

    d Linda got up early _____ she wanted to go for a run.

    e Pop took his pullover with him _____ he felt cold.

3. **Turn these sentences round to put the subordinate clause first. Don't forget the punctuation!**

    a We were woken up when there was a loud hammering on the cabin door.

    _____

    b She found it harder and harder to run because of the pelting rain.

    _____

    c Father moved back into the crowd once he had helped us into the lifeboats.

    _____

0			12	Total
Tough	OK	Got it!		12

Active and passive 1

Grammar | **Lesson 10**

> **Active** sentences tell us that someone (subject) is doing (verb) something (object).
> **Active** means doing something: John **chased** Tim.
> **Passive** sentences tell us that something (object) is being done (verb) to someone (subject).
> **Passive** means letting it happen: Tim **was chased by** John.

1. Write whether these sentences are active or passive.

   a Geoff drove Kelly home.   _____

   b Kelly was driven home by Geoff.   _____

   c Baby Cara was being fed by Mum.   _____

   d Mum fed baby Cara.   _____

   e Dad is mowing the lawn.   _____

   f The lawn is being mowed by Dad.   _____

2. Who was doing what to whom in these active sentences?

	subject	verb	object
a Jane caught the ball.			
b Aaron took some photographs.			
c Jamil rode this bike yesterday.			
d Emily made a chocolate cake.			

3. What was being done by whom in these passive sentences?

	subject	verb	object
a The ball was caught by Jane.			
b Some photographs were taken by Aaron.			
c This bike was ridden by Jamil yesterday.			
d The chocolate cake was made by Emily.			

0			14	Total
Tough	OK	Got it!		/14

Lesson 11 Grammar

Active and passive 2

> Active sentences can be changed into passive sentences, and passive sentences can be changed into active sentences.
> **Active**   Bella hit the ball.
> **Passive**   The ball was hit by Bella.

1. **Change these passive sentences into active sentences.**

   a The school was told about the new building by the head teacher.
   _____

   b The Junior League was won at Denby, North Carolina by Henfield School.
   _____

   c The winning horse was ridden by an unknown jockey.
   _____

   d All the fruit juice had been drunk by the team.
   _____

2. **Change these active sentences into passive ones.**

   a Joe will drive Emma home. _____

   b The dog bit a boy. _____

   c The policeman chased the thief. _____

   d The dog ate the remains of the pie. _____

3. **Instructions are written using active sentences. Imagine you watched someone following these instructions. Write what they did.** *(4 marks)*

   Put a teaspoon of salt into $\frac{1}{4}$ litre of water. Stir the mixture and pour it into a bowl. Place the bowl on the window sill in the sunlight. Leave the dish there until all the water has evaporated and then leave it for a further 24 hours before examining it.

   A teaspoon of salt was put into $\frac{1}{4}$ litre of water. _____
   _____
   _____
   _____

0			12	Total
Tough	OK	Got it!		/12

Colons and semicolons Punctuation Lesson 12

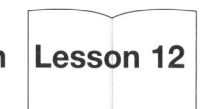

> **Colons** are used to introduce lists, quotations and explanations:
>   He bought: eggs, flour, sugar and milk. His reason was this: the birthday cake.
>
> **Semicolons** have several uses. The most common ones are:
> - in **complex lists**: He has frogs and bats; snails and mice; pigs and cows.
> - to **link sentences** instead of conjunctions: Mice eat cheese; cows eat grass.
> - to **precede conjunctions** such as: however, nevertheless, that is to say.

1. **Write the missing colons and commas, if required, in these sentences.**

   a The list of ingredients included chicken onions mushrooms tomatoes and seasoning.

   b The characters in the story included Dorothy the lion the scarecrow and the tin man.

   c I am away on the following days 3 March 22 April 8 and 15 May.

   d Your duties to sweep the stairs and to dust the hall.

2. **Write the missing colons in these explanations.**

   a There was only one thing they could do hide.

   b The information had just come through the contract was signed.

   c The exam results were on the notice board they had all passed.

3. **Write the missing colons and semicolons in these complex lists.**

   a She sent cards to Mike in Melbourne Laura in Perth Ravi in California and Heidi in Iowa.

   b The chef needed strips of raw chicken thin slices of courgettes some bamboo shoots and oil.

4. **Use semicolons to join the two main clauses in these sentences.**

   a Some people are good at games some are not.

   b A few of us wanted to go to India the rest wanted to go to Thailand.

   c She had been brought up in France but they still considered her to be English.

5. **Write semicolons before the conjunctions in these sentences.**

   a She was encouraged to run every day however, it was not compulsory.

   b No one stood over him while he worked nevertheless, he always tried his hardest.

0			14	Total
Tough	OK	Got it!		/14

Lesson 13 Punctuation

Hyphens and dashes

> **Hyphens** can be used:
> - to form **compound** words:
> steam-roller
> - to clarify the **meaning** of some words:
> He saw a man-eating tiger. (Not a man eating tiger for dinner)
> - to **split** the word at the end of a syllable if the whole word cannot be written on one line:
> amuse-
> ment.
>
> **Dashes** are used to show breaks in sentences in informal writing and for emphasis:
> There were five cats on the sofa – and they were all black.

1. **Put the missing hyphens into these compound words.**

   a hanggliding _____   b sisterinlaw _____

   c windowshopping _____   d weightbearing _____

2. **Put the missing hyphens into these sentences.**

   a The passers by looked at the new poster.

   b Peru is a Spanish speaking country.

   c The alarm made a high pitched sound.

   d The baby sitter arrived at 7.30pm.

3. **Put hyphens into these words to show sensible places to split them if they each had to be split across two lines.**

   a marvellous _____   b opportunity _____

4. **Use dashes to emphasise a point being made in each of these sentences.**

   a He had originally thought there was no point in running but he changed his mind!
   _____

   b I'll say it again I don't think you're listening.
   _____

Commas and brackets

Punctuation — Lesson 14

> **Commas** are used to add a comment, an aside, in a sentence:
>
> We went to St Paul's, in London, to see a concert.
>
> **Brackets** come in pairs and can be used:
>
> - to insert a useful (but not essential) piece of information:
>   Charles Kingsley (1819–75) wrote *The Water Babies*.
>
> - to mark off numerals, alternatives and abbreviations:
>   London Heathrow Airport (LHR).

1. **Use commas to separate the aside from the main sentence.**

   a We went to Winchester in Hampshire to see the cathedral.

   b It was on balance a pretty good idea.

   c They had arrived at long last in Edinburgh.

   d Alan Paton the prize-winning South African novelist wrote *Cry the Beloved Country*.

   e Now she thought it is time to leave.

2. **Put brackets into these sentences to enclose the non-essential information.**

   a Michael Foreman born 1938 is a prolific illustrator and author.

   b The discoverer of penicillin Alexander Fleming was Scottish.

   c Claude Monet's painting *Impression: Sunrise* 1872 gave its name to Impressionism.

   d London UK is one of the largest cities in the world.

3. **Put brackets round the alternative ways of writing the words.**

   a Mark claims he saw an Unidentified Flying Object UFO last night.

   b The English we are taught in schools is from the National Literacy Strategy NLS.

   c The fee is ten pounds £10.

Lesson 15 Comprehension

Classic fiction

> This is a short extract from a **classic novel** by Charles Dickens. It uses a lot of **dialogue** and **colloquial language**.

Read the extract and then answer the questions.

"Hold your noise!" cried a terrible voice, as a man started up from among the graves at the side of the church porch. "Keep still, you little devil, or I'll cut your throat!"

A fearful man, all in coarse grey, with a great iron ring on his leg. A man with no hat, and with broken shoes, and with an old rag tied round his head. A man whose teeth chattered in his head as he seized me by the chin.

"O! Don't cut my throat, sir," I pleaded in terror. "Pray don't do it, sir."

"Tell us your name!" said the man. "Quick!"

"Pip, sir."

"Show us where you live," said the man. "Point out the place!"

I pointed to where our village lay, on the flat in-shore among the alder-trees and pollards, a mile or more from the church.

The man, after looking at me for a moment, turned me upside down, and emptied my pockets. There was nothing in them but a piece of bread.

"You young dog," said the man, licking his lips, "what fat cheeks you ha' got. Where's your mother?"

"There, sir!" said I.

He started, made a short run, and stopped and looked over his shoulder.

"There, sir!" I timidly explained. " 'Also Georgiana'. That's my mother."

"Oh!" said he, coming back. "And is that your father lying alongside your mother?"

"Yes, sir," said I; "him too; 'late of this parish'."

"Ha!" he muttered then, considering. "Who d'ye live with – supposin' you're kindly let to live, which I han't made up my mind about?"

"My sister, sir – Mrs. Joe Gargery – wife of Joe Gargery, the blacksmith, sir."

"Blacksmith, eh?" said he. And looked down at his leg. "Now lookee here," he said, "the question being whether you're to be let to live. You know what a file is? And you know what provisions are?"

"Yes, sir."

"You get me a file." He tilted me upside down. "And you get me food." He tilted me again. "You bring 'em both to me." He tilted me again. "Or I'll have your heart and liver out."

I said that I would get him the file, and I would get him what broken bits of food I could, and I would come to him at the Battery, early in the morning.

"Say Lord strike you dead if you don't!" said the man.

"Goo-good night, sir," I faltered.

Circle the right answer.

1. **The story takes place in:**

   a field   a church   a prison   a graveyard

2. **On his leg the prisoner had:**

   a boot   a plaster   an iron ring   some grey cloth

3. **Pip's sister is married to:**

   a teacher   a farmer   a blacksmith   a prison guard

4. **'Late of this parish' means:**

   gone away   now dead   living in the village   always late

5. **Write down six things you know about the prisoner from this passage.** *(6 marks)*

   _____

   _____

6. **What two things did the prisoner want? Why was each one so important to him?**

   (2 marks)

   _____

   _____

7. **Why did the prisoner start to run when Pip said his mother was 'There, sir'?**

   _____

   _____

8. **How did Pip feel during the meeting? Find two sentences that explain this.** *(2 marks)*

   _____

   _____

0			15	Total
Tough	OK	Got it!		15

Lesson 16 Comprehension

Non-chronological reports

> Non-chronological reports are **information texts** that do not follow a time sequence. Non-fiction books, information leaflets and tourist brochures are all examples of non-chronological reports. They tend to:
> - have a clear **introductory paragraph** and a **concluding comment**
> - follow a **clear** and **logical order** in the main paragraphs
> - offer **facts**, not opinions
> - be written in a **formal** style and in the **present** tense (except for historical reports)
> - use **connectives** – for example to show comparisons or additional comments
> - use precise, **descriptive** and **technical** language.

Read this non-chronological report, then answer the questions.

The Lake District is a popular National Park. More and more people enjoy its fantastic scenery each year, due to increasing numbers of car owners and improvements to local roads and motorways. This, however, is placing an ever-increasing pressure on this beautiful and valuable environment.

Traffic jams in and around the Lake District create air pollution. Parking facilities at most tourist sites are overflowing in peak season causing visitors to park on grass verges which, in turn, causes soil erosion. Litter is also a problem, although many bins are provided and people are encouraged to take their litter home.

Activities such as hiking, camping and mountain biking cause severe footpath erosion. Visitors often leave the designated trails, risking nesting birds and animals being disturbed, vegetation being destroyed and water courses becoming polluted.

In addition, the traditional hill farming of the Lake District has effects on the landscape. Grazing sheep keep the grass short and eat other vegetation, including young saplings. The difficulty faced now is how to preserve the beauty of this area without lowering the enjoyment of visitors or impairing the livelihoods of local farmers.

1. **What is the Lake District?** _____

2. **Give three reasons why so many people come to the Lake District now.**

    a _____

    b _____

    c _____

3. **List six key problems caused by visitor numbers:**

   a _____

   b _____

   c _____

   d _____

   e _____

   f _____

4. **Give four examples of technical vocabulary used in this report.**

   a _____ b _____

   c _____ d _____

5. **Circle the connectives used in this report.**

6. **What is the main purpose of this non-chronological report?**

   _____

   _____

7. **Which sentence introduces the main focus of this report?**

   _____

8. **Is the information in the report organised in a logical order? Explain your answer.**

   _____

   _____

9. **Does the author express any personal opinions? Explain your answer.**

   _____

   _____

0			19	Total
Tough	OK	Got it!		/19

How am I doing?

1. **Underline the unstressed vowels in these words.**

   a Wednesday   b government   c chimney   d geography

   e cupboard   f Saturday   g skeleton   h raspberry

   i parallel   j constable   k lavatory   l library

2. **Underline the root words in these words.**

   a classify   b artistically   c longevity   d ageism   e magnetise

   f childishness   g enjoyment   h unhappily   i impossibility   j immobility

3. **Use a word beginning with the given prefix to complete these sentences.**

   a They lived in a sub_____ of London.

   b She spoke fluent French so she was able to trans_____ the document.

   c A teacher was sent to super_____ the children doing the exam.

   d We need to post_____ our visit.

4. **What are the meanings of these Latin prefixes?**

   a bi _____   b tri _____   c quad _____   d dec _____

5. **Use a word beginning with one of the prefixes above to provide the answers.**

   a Something you ride on with two wheels. _____

   b A four-sided yard. _____

   c A period of ten years. _____

   d In geometry – a three-sided shape. _____

6. **Choose a connective to complete these sentences.**

   whenever   but   so   on the other hand   although

   a We could go for a walk; _____, we could go to the shops.

   b _____ she left her old teddy bear, Jan took her new book with her.

   c All my family are blond _____ I am a brunette.

   d He kept his kit handy _____ he could grab it when it was time to leave.

   e _____ you feel like going, just let me know.

7. **Fill in the spaces with one of these prepositions. Use each preposition once.**

   across   along   about   inside   against   through   into

   a It will be _____ four o'clock by the time we get there.

   b We ran _____ the pavement and out _____ the gate.

   c Carole was leaning _____ the gate waiting for me.

   d We went _____ the house and _____ the hallway _____ the kitchen.

8. **Rewrite these sentences so that the nouns, adjectives and verbs agree.**

   a A stitches in times saved nines. _____

   b We had bean on toasts for tea. _____

   c We clap our hand when we see the clowns. _____

   d Too many cook spoils the broths. _____

9. **Use conjunctions to complete these sentences.**

   a _____ you can have your pudding, you must eat your main course.

   b _____ it was time to go, we still were not ready.

   d _____ Mum had closed the shop, we couldn't go home.

10. **Change these sentences from passive to active.**

    a The pancake had been eaten by Charlie. _____

    b The shoelaces of Anna were tied by Mum. _____

    c A new hockey stick was bought by Lois. _____

11. **Rewrite these sentences putting in the missing commas, colons or semicolons.**

    a Marc's bag held the following his homework a book two biros a pencil and a rubber.
    _____

    b The house was sold they were finally moving to France.
    _____

12. **Write the missing hyphens.**

    a Eddie was standard bearer at the presentation.

    b Montreal is the second largest French speaking city in the world.

    c The cries of cock a doodle do filled the air.

Total /58

Lesson 17 Spelling

Unstressed letters

Spelling words with unstressed letters can be made easier using these suggestions:
1. Break a word down into **syllables** and pronounce each one: personal – per / son / al.
2. Think of **other words** that come from the **same root**: medicine – medic.
3. Look for **words within words**: carpentry – car-pen-try.

QUICK TIP!
Words can have more than one unstressed letter.

1. **Split these words into syllables, then underline the unstressed letters.**

   a Tuesday _____   b Saturday _____

   c dietary _____   d flavour _____

   e victory _____   f savoury _____

2. **Underline the unstressed letters. Which word or words within the words below could help you remember the unstressed letters?**

   a mathematics _____   b cupboard _____

   c carpet _____   d portable _____

3. **Rewrite these words correctly, putting in the missing unstressed letters.**

   a Wensdy _____   b hanbag _____

   c rasbry _____   d enviruhmunt _____

   e extruh _____   f govuhmunt _____

   g compny _____   h poisnus _____

   i jewllry _____   j diffrunt _____

4. **Use one of the words on this page to complete these sentences.**

   a Mum went out to the shops and left her _____ behind.

   b Deadly nightshade is so called because it is _____.

   c The _____ rule our country.

   d How many _____ animals can you see?

0			24	Total
Tough	OK	Got it!		/24

Prefixes

Spelling Lesson 18

> If you can recognise a **prefix** in an unfamiliar word, it can help you to **spell** the word correctly and make it possible for you to **guess** the meaning of the unknown word.

1. Link these prefixes with their meanings.

   a audi   **b** micro   **c** tele   **d** duo   **e** hydro   **f** port   **g** prim

   distant   water   hear   carry   first   small   two

2. Read the definitions and add the correct prefix to complete each word.

   a If an object is easy to carry it is _____able.

   b A _____ makes tiny objects look bigger.

   c Blue, red and yellow are _____ colours.

   d A _____ is part of a computer.

3. Complete each of these sets of words with a prefix from question 1.

   a _____graph   _____phone   _____vision   _____scope

   b _____ence   _____torium   _____tion   _____ble

   c _____ary   _____ate   _____itive   _____acy

4. Write one word that you know that begins with each of these prefixes:

   a tele _____   **b** micro _____

   c auto _____   **d** anti _____

   e sub _____   **f** extra _____

   g inter _____   **h** semi _____

0			22
Tough	OK		Got it!

Total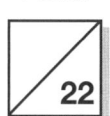

Lesson 19 Spelling

Spelling strategies 1

> Seeing that words belong in families can help with spelling.
> If you can spell **probable**, you can easily spell **probably, improbable, probability**.
> If you can spell **care**, you can easily spell **careful, careless, carelessly**.

1. Use both a prefix and a suffix to make a new word from each of the words below. Choose from the following each time. The first one has been done for you.

   Prefixes: ir, im, in, un   Suffixes: ful, ness, able, ly

   a important   _unimportantly_   b regular   _____

   c frequent   _____   d kind   _____

   e move   _____   f touch   _____

   g polite   _____   h success   _____

2. Make two more family words for each of the following. You may need to change the end of the original word. The first one has been done for you.

   a sensitive   _insensitive_   _sensitivity_

   b accept   _____   _____

   c memory   _____   _____

   d guilt   _____   _____

   e courage   _____   _____

   f conscious   _____   _____

   g critic   _____   _____

   h relevant   _____   _____

   i meaning   _____   _____

   j friend   _____   _____

   k different   _____   _____

   l peace   _____   _____

0			18
Tough	OK	Got it!	

Total

Spelling strategies 2

Spelling Lesson 20

A number of words have the same root word before prefixes, suffixes, plurals and other letter clusters (such as **end, ation, ance, ly, ing** and **ess**) are added to extend their meaning.

For example, like: likely, liking, likeness, unlikely

1. **Use the root word to find three family words.**

   a commend _____ _____ _____

   b exist _____ _____ _____

   c comfort _____ _____ _____

   d special _____ _____ _____

   e define _____ _____ _____

2. **Use one of the family words above to complete these sentences.**

   a Tom ran as fast as he could. He was _____ going to be late.

   b Her birthday was going to be an _____ nice day.

   c James was _____ for his hard work.

   d Many species were on the earth before the _____ of humans.

   e It was _____ to cuddle a hot-water bottle in bed.

3. **Write the root word in these words.**

   a incomparable _____

   b intensely _____

   c unhelpful _____

   d immoveable

0			14
Tough	OK	Got it!	

Total /14

27

Lesson 21 Spelling

Homophones 2

> **A reminder** – **homophones** are made from two words:
> **homo** means **same**   **phone** means **sound**
>
> This means that they sound the same but are spelt differently and have different meanings:
> It was all in the **past**. He **passed** her by.

1. Link the homophones that sound the same.

   a cereal   license   b steak   passed

   c descent   serial   d draft   stake

   e licence   dissent   f past   draught

2. Use these homophones to complete the sentences.

   steal/steel   not/knot   male/mail   practice/practise

   a It was a _____ postman who delivered the _____.

   b A doctor has a _____ where he can _____ medicine.

   c Barry could _____ tie a _____ in his shoelaces.

   d Robbers planned to _____ some _____ from the factory.

3. Fill in the correct homophones.

   a She didn't _____ the answer.   b Mum's answer was _____.

   c He hadn't _____ an inch taller. d He let out a _____.

   e The grass was wet with _____.   f The rent was _____.

   g There was a fire in the _____. h It looked _____.

0			18
Tough	OK	Got it!	

Total

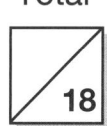

Homophones 3

Spelling | Lesson 22

> A **homophone** can be a **noun** (the **name** of something), a **verb** (a **doing** word) or an **adjective** which **describes** a noun. Knowing what they are helps with spelling.
>
> **House** is a noun, a place where people live.
> **Aid** is a verb and means to go to someone's aid (help) when they are having difficulty with something.
> **Beautiful** is an adjective which describes how lovely something is.

1. Link the verbs and nouns that sound the same.

	Verbs	Nouns		Verbs	Nouns
a	tied	nose	b	ate	meat
c	guessed	tide	d	might	eight
e	knows	guest	f	meet	mite

2. Use these homophones to complete the sentences.

   throne/thrown   maid/made   miner/minor

   a His father worked underground, he was a _____.

   b The _____ came in and _____ the beds.

   c The queen sits on the _____.

   d If you are under eighteen you are a _____.

   e He had _____ his jacket down on the ground.

3. Write the correct spelling for the adjectives in these sentences.

   a Lorna had two _____ dogs. (livley, lively)

   b Valerie is an _____ cook. (excellent, excellant)

   c She had her own _____ radio. (portible, portable)

   d It was an _____ item in her school bag. (essential/essenshal)

0			15
Tough		OK	Got it!

Total /15

Lesson 23 | Grammar

Active and passive 3

> Sentences are usually written in the **active voice** – showing that the subject **performs** the action.
>   **I sold** the house.
> **Passive** sentences are used when it is more important to **emphasise the action** that is being done or **the person or thing it is done to**, rather than who is performing the action.
>   The house **was sold**.

1. **Underline the verbs in these sentences and say whether they are active or passive.**

   a Sue signed all the letters. _____

   b The room was cluttered with books and papers. _____

   c Mike invited Shereen to go to a party. _____

   d Ali was sitting on a bench with Conrad. _____

   e They had been warned by their father to keep away from next door's dog. _____

2. **Change these sentences from active to passive ones. The first one is done for you.**

   a Dad kept all his tools in the shed. _All Dad's tools were kept in the shed._

   b Robin propped his bike against the fence. _____

   c Mum's shopping filled six bags. _____

   d Jill tidied the notice board. _____

   e Grandpa swept the front path. _____

3. **Turn these passive sentences into active ones, removing any unnecessary words.**

   a The drums were being played by Mick, and the cymbals were being played by Lisa.
   _____

   b The shirt bought by Sara was a pink one, and the shirt bought by Claire was a blue one.
   _____

   c It was when the window cleaner's ladder fell over that Ruth was struck on the head.
   _____

   d They were told by Dr Barnett to take Raj to hospital.
   _____

Formal language

Grammar | Lesson 24

> **Formal language** is used for instructions, commands, reports, explanatory text and official letters. It is written in an **impersonal style** – the author's voice is not heard and a specific reader is not identified.
>
> **Passive sentences** and **imperative verbs** – ones giving orders or commands – are often used:
>
> Smoking is not allowed. Keep to the left.

1. Match the formal and informal styles of these notices.

Formal	Informal
a Keep off the grass.	Sorry, but we have to charge for all breakages.
b Parking is for permit holders only.	Please don't walk on our grass.
c Breakages must be paid for.	You can't park here without a permit.

2. Rewrite these requests in a formal style, using imperative verbs forms.

   a We would like you all to park on the left.
   _____

   b You can't bring children in here.
   _____

   c Please don't talk in the corridor, children.
   _____

3. Rewrite this note using formal language. *(4 marks)*

   Hi Sarah!
   In case you don't know, your electricity is going off later, probably around 10am. Should be back on at about 4pm.
   Cheers!
   The electricity guy

   Dear Ms Jones _____
   _____
   _____
   _____

   QUICK TIP!
   The date is always given on formal letters.

0 — Tough — OK — Got it! — 10

Total /10

31

Lesson 25 Grammar

Complex sentences

> In complex sentences the main and subordinate clauses are joined by a **subordinating conjunction** or phrase, such as:
>
> until   even though   after   since   although
>
> The subordinate clause can be placed **before**, **within** or **after** the main clause, but must be introduced by a conjunction:
>
> She wanted to go, **if** it were possible, to the theme park.

1. **Circle the conjunctions and underline the subordinate clauses below.**

   a Before you sit down to dinner, go and wash your hands.

   b After pitching our tents, we started to climb the hill.

   c The taller boy, who was wearing a green tracksuit, turned to face me.

   d The London Marathon, which is run by people of all ages, is 26 miles long.

2. **What separates the clauses in the sentences above?** _____

3. **Choose a suitable subordinating conjunction to complete these sentences.**

   although   since   because   until   after   before

   a She hadn't seen Pam _____ last November.

   b _____ it was a wet day, Nick decided to stay indoors.

   c They arrived early, _____ the rest of the group.

   d _____ the parcel arrives, I will have to wait at home.

   e _____ the match, they had tea with the other team.

   f _____ there was a traffic jam, they still arrived on time.

0			11	Total
	Tough	OK	Got it!	/11

No Nonsense
English
10–11 years

Parents' notes

What your child will learn from this book

Bond No Nonsense will help your child to understand and become more confident at English. This book features the main English objectives covered by your child's class teacher during the school year. It provides clear, straightforward teaching and learning of the essentials in a rigorous, step-by-step way.

This book begins with some **handwriting practice**. Encourage your child to complete this carefully and to continue writing neatly throughout the book.

The four types of lessons provided are:
Spelling – these cover spelling rules and strategies.
Grammar – these cover word types and sentence construction.
Punctuation – these cover punctuation marks and their rules.
Comprehension – these cover reading different types of text and comprehension questions.

How you can help

Following a few simple guidelines will ensure that your child gets the best from this book:
- Explain that the book will help your child become confident in their English work.
- If your child has difficulty reading the text on the page or understanding a question, do provide help.
- Encourage your child to complete all the exercises in a lesson. You can mark the work using this answer section. Your child can record their own impressions of the work using the 'How did I do?' feature.

- The 'How am I doing?' sections provide a further review of progress.

A1

Bond No Nonsense 10–11 years Answers

1 Unstressed vowels p4
1 a fatt**e**ning b dand**e**lion c mini**a**ture d int**e**rest e astron**o**my
   f aband**o**n g lett**u**ce h ben**e**fit i journ**a**list j mathem**a**tics
2 a tel**e**vision b parli**a**ment c veg**e**table d conson**a**nt e cem**e**tery
   f ov**e**n g sign**a**ture h med**i**cine i mus**c**le j gramm**a**r
3 a sep**a**rate b defin**i**te c inter**e**sting d teleph**o**ne e nuis**a**nce
   f secr**e**tary g misch**ie**vous h temper**a**ture i lem**o**nade
4 February lottery history
   January stationery factory
   boundary jewellery category
   stationary battery
   voluntary veterinary

2 Word roots p5
1 a digest b cipher c prefer d hyphen
   e correspond f integrate g concept h learn
2 Possible answers include:
   a fireman, fireside, fireplace
   b committee, commitment, committed
   c specialist, specialise, especially
   d fortune, fortieth, fortnight
   e safely, safety, safeguard
3 a submerge b postscript c transform d superfluous
   e interrupt f contradict g prepare

3 Suffixes p6
1 a commandment, commandant
   b ignorant, ignorance
   c informant, informal
   d attendant, attendance
2 a substantial b commercial
   c partial d financial
   e confidential f artificial
   g racial h provincial
   i denial
3 a adorable b noticeable
   c enjoyable d sensible
   e changeable f forcible
4 a preferable, preference b musical, musician
   c breakable, breakage

4 Connectives p7
1 a then b after c so d because
2 a whereas b however c therefore d whatever
   e whoever f meanwhile g moreover
3 a nevertheless b insofar
4 time: meanwhile / afterwards
   sequence: secondly / lastly
   logic: therefore / so

5 Homophones 1 p8
1 a aisle – isle b aloud – allowed
   c bawl – ball d ascent – assent
   e altar – alter f bridal – bridle
2 a principals, principles b heard, herd
   c father, further d guessed, guests
3 a who's b Whose
   c led d lead
   e passed f past
   g desert h dessert

6 'ough' words p9
1 a ruff b awt c throo
   d thoh e plow f coff
2 a through b cough c ought
   d though e plough f rough
3 a thorough b through
   c though d thorough

7 Prepositions p10
1 a off b across c through d around e up
   f during g under h behind/in i on
2 a in spite of b by means of c in accordance with d because of

8 Conventions p11
1 a a trolley b an orange c some pears d a basket
   e some new shoes f an object g an apple h a road
2 a some yellow bikes b those six pencils
   c a nice house d an empty case
   e my own bed f the good old days
3 a Ivan will see her tomorrow.
   b I went yesterday.
   c Len will run next Sunday.
   d Mary danced last Saturday.
   e Ivan will play on his Gameboy tomorrow.
4 a It is fun to go on holiday. b I like playing in the park.
   c Bob stayed in bed late this d Tom tripped over a stone yesterday morning.
   e Lena swam several races last Wednesday.
   f A leopard cannot change his spots.
   g You must be home before seven o'clock.
   h The early bird catches the worm.

9 Complex sentences p12
1 a (If we hurry,) we will catch the next bus.
   b (When the bell rang,) we went out into the playground.
   c He turned off the lights, (before he went out.)
   d (To keep the Mongols out of China,) the Emperor built the Great Wall.
2 a Since / Because / When b after c until / even though
   d because e in case
3 a When there was a loud hammering on the cabin door, we were woken up.
   b Because of the pelting rain, she found it harder and harder to run.
   c Once he had helped us into the lifeboats, Father moved back into the crowd.

10 Active and passive 1 p13
1 a active b passive c passive d active e active f passive
2 a Jane (s) caught (v) ball (o)
   b Aaron (s) took (v) photographs (o)
   c Jamil (s) rode (v) bike (o)
   d Emily (s) made (v) chocolate cake (o)
3 a Jane (s) was caught (v) ball (o)
   b Aaron (s) were taken (v) photographs (o)
   c Jamil (s) was ridden (v) bike (o)
   d Emily (s) was made (v) chocolate cake (o)

11 Active and passive 2 p14
1 a The head teacher told the school about the new building.
   b Henfield School won the Junior League at Denby, North Carolina.
   c An unknown jockey rode the winning horse.
   d The team drank all the fruit juice.
2 a Emma will be driven home by Joe.
   b A boy was bitten by the dog.
   c The thief was chased by the policeman.
   d The remains of the pie were eaten by the dog.
3 A teaspoon of salt was put into $\frac{1}{4}$ litre of water. The mixture was stirred and poured into a bowl. The bowl was placed on the window sill in the sunlight. The dish was left there until all the water had evaporated and left for a further 24 hours before the dish was examined.

12 Colons and semicolons p15
1 a The list of ingredients included: chicken, onions, mushrooms, tomatoes and seasoning.
   b The characters in the story included: Dorothy, the lion, the scarecrow and the tin man.
   c I am away on the following days: 3 March, 22 April, 8 and 15 May.
   d Your duties: to sweep the stairs and to dust the hall.
2 a There was only one thing they could do: hide.
   b The information had just come through: the contract was signed.
   c The exam results were on the notice board: they had all passed.
3 a She sent cards to: Mike in Melbourne; Laura in Perth; Ravi in California and Heidi in Iowa.
   b The chef needed: strips of raw chicken; thin slices of courgettes; some bamboo shoots and oil.
4 a Some people are good at games; some are not.
   b A few of us wanted to go to India; the rest wanted to go to Thailand.
   c She had been brought up in France; but they still considered her to be English.
5 a She was encouraged to run every day; however, it was not compulsory.
   b No one stood over him while he worked; nevertheless, he always tried his hardest.

13 Hyphens and dashes p16
1 a hang-gliding b sister-in-law c window-shopping d weight-bearing
2 a passers-by b Spanish-speaking c high-pitched d baby-sitter
3 a marvel-lous b oppor-tunity
4 He had originally thought there was no point in running – but he changed his mind!
5 I'll say it again – I don't think you're listening.

14 Commas and brackets p17
1 a We went to Winchester, in Hampshire, to see …
   b It was, on balance, a …
   c They had arrived, at long last, …
   d Alan Paton, the prize-winning South African novelist, wrote …
   e Now, she thought, it …
2 a Michael Foreman (born 1938) is …
   b The discoverer of penicillin (Alexander Fleming) was …
   c Claude Monet's painting *Impression: Sunrise* (1872) gave …
   d London (UK) is …
3 a Mark claims he saw an Unidentified Flying Object (UFO) last night.
   b The English we are taught in schools is from the National Literacy Strategy (NLS).
   c The fee is ten pounds (£10).

15 Classic fiction p18
1 a graveyard
2 an iron ring
3 a blacksmith
4 now dead
5 Any six of the following: he was a fearful man / he wore coarse grey / he had an iron ring on his leg / he had no hat / he had broken shoes / his teeth chattered / he was cold / he was hungry.
6 Some food because he was very hungry / a file to get the iron ring off his leg.
7 The prisoner thought that Pip's mother was nearby and would catch him.
8 Pip was terrified. Phrases such as the following explain this: "O! Don't cut my throat, sir!" I pleaded in terror. / "There, sir!" I timidly explained. / "Goo-good night, sir," I faltered.

16 Non-chronological reports p20
1 A National Park
2 a It has fantastic scenery.
   b There is an increasing number of car owners.
   c There have been improvements to local roads and motorways.
3 Possible answers include:
   air pollution caused by traffic jams / overflowing car parks / soil erosion caused by parking in verges / litter / footpath erosion caused by outdoor activities / risk to birds and animals because visitors leave paths / pollution of water courses / grazing sheep eat young saplings.
4 Any four from: air pollution / soil erosion / designated trails / vegetation / water courses.
5 due to / however / also / although / In addition
6 The main purpose of this report is to highlight the damaging effect visitors and local farm life are having on the environment in the Lake District.
7 The last sentence of the first paragraph: 'This, however, is placing an ever-increasing pressure on this beautiful and valuable environment.'
8 Yes, the information is presented in a logical order. The first paragraph introduces the topic. The following paragraphs explore the issues in more detail, drawing to a close in the concluding statement of fact.
9 No, the author does not express any personal opinions. This is a non-chronological report which lists the facts of the situation without introducing the voice of the author.

How am I doing? p22

1. a Wednes<u>day</u>   b govern<u>ment</u>   c chim<u>ney</u>   d ge<u>o</u>graphy
   e cupb<u>o</u>ard   f Satur<u>day</u>   g skelet<u>on</u>   h rasp<u>ber</u>ry
   i p<u>ar</u>allel   j const<u>a</u>ble   k lav<u>a</u>tory   l libr<u>ar</u>y
2. a <u>classify</u>   b <u>artistically</u>   c <u>longevity</u>   d <u>age</u>ism
   e <u>magnetise</u>   f <u>child</u>ishness   g <u>en</u>joyment   h <u>un</u>happily
   i <u>im</u>possibility   j <u>im</u>mobility
3. a suburb   b translate   c supervise   d postpone
4. a two   b three   c four   d ten
5. a bicycle   b quadrangle   c decade   d triangle
6. a on the other hand   b Although   c but   d so
   e Whenever
7. a about   b along / through   c against   d inside / across / into
8. a A stitch in time saves nine.
   b We had beans on toast for tea.
   c We clapped our hands when we saw the clowns.
   d Too many cooks spoil the broth.
9. a Before   b Although   c Until
10. a Charlie had eaten the pancake.   b Mum tied Anna's shoelaces.
    c Lois bought a new hockey stick.
11. a Marc's bag held the following: his homework; a book; two biros; a pencil and a rubber.
    b The house was sold; they were finally moving to France.
12. a Eddie was standard-bearer at the presentation.
    b Montreal is the second largest French-speaking city in the world.
    c The cries of cock-a-doodle-do filled the air.

17 Unstressed letters p24

1. a Tues / d<u>a</u>y   b Sat / <u>ur</u> / d<u>a</u>y   c di / et / <u>a</u> / ry   d fla / v<u>our</u>
   e vic / t<u>or</u> / y   f sav / <u>our</u> / y
2. a mathematics: the, he, hem, them   b cupboard: cup, up / board, boar, oar
   c carpet: pet   d portable: tab, table, able
3. a Wednesday   b handbag   c raspberry   d environment
   e extra   f government   g company   h poisonous
   i jewellery   j different
4. a handbag   b poisonous   c government   d different

18 Prefixes p25

1. a audi / hear   b micro / small   c tele / distant   d duo / two
   e hydro / water   f port / carry   g prim / first
2. a portable   b telescope   c primary   d microchip
3. a tele   b audi   c prim
4. Possible answers include:
   a telephone   b microphone   c autograph   d anticlockwise
   e submarine   f extraterrestrial   g international   h semicircular

19 Spelling strategies 1 p26

1. b irregularly   c infrequently   d unkindness/unkindly
   e immovable   f untouchable   g impolitely
   h unsuccessful
2. Possible answers include:
   b acceptable, unacceptable   c memorable, memorise
   d guilty, guiltless   e courageous, courageously
   f consciously, consciousness, unconscious   g critic, critically
   h irrelevant, relevancy   i meaningful, meaningless
   j friendly, friendliness   k indifferent, differently
   l peaceful, peacemaker

20 Spelling strategies 2 p27

1. a commended, commendable, commendation
   b existence, existing, existed
   c comforted, comforting, uncomfortable
   d especially, specialist, specialism
   e definitely, definition, indefinite
2. a definitely   b especially   c commended
   d existence   e comforting
3. a compare   b tense   c help   d move

21 Homophones 2 p28

1. a cereal, serial   b steak, stake   c descent, dissent
   d draft, draught   e licence, license   f past, passed
2. a male, mail   b practice, practise
   c not, knot   d steal, steel
3. a know   b no   c grown   d groan
   e dew   f due   g grate   h great

22 Homophones 3 p29

1. a tied, tide   b ate, eight   c guessed, guest
   d might, mite   e knows, nose   f meet, meat
2. a miner   b maid, made   c throne
   d minor   e thrown
3. a lively   b excellent   c essential
   c portable

23 Active and passive 3 p30

1. a signed / active   b was cluttered / passive   c invited / active
   d was sitting / active   e had been warned / passive
2. b The bike was propped against the fence by Robin.
   c Six bags were filled with Mum's shopping.
   d The notice board was tidied by Jill.
   e The front path was swept by Grandpa.
3. a Mick played the drums and Lisa (played) the cymbals.
   b Sara bought a pink shirt and Claire (bought) a blue one.
   c The window cleaner's ladder struck Ruth on the head when it fell over.
   d Dr Barnett told them to take Raj to hospital.

24 Formal language p31

1. a Keep off the grass. / Please don't walk on our grass.
   b Parking for permit holders only. / You can't park here without a permit.
   c Breakages must be paid for. / Sorry, but we have to charge for all breakages.
2. Possible answers include:
   a Park on the left.
   b Children may not be brought inside.
   c Children are not allowed to talk in the corridor.
3. Possible answers include:
   Dear Ms Jones

You may be unaware that from 10am this morning, your electricity will be temporarily disconnected. Your supply should be reconnected by approximately 4pm this afternoon.
We apologise for any inconvenience this may cause.
Yours sincerely,
Southern Electricity Board

25 Complex sentences p32

1. a conjunction: Before / subordinate clause: Before you sit down to dinner
   b conjunction: After / subordinate clause: After pitching our tents
   c conjunction: who / subordinate clause: who was wearing a green tracksuit.
   d conjunction: which / subordinate clause: which is run by people of all ages
2. commas
3. a since   b Because   c before   d Until
   e After   f Although

26 Clauses 1 p33

1. a which he went to   b that you wrote
   c for whom I play   d whose thumb is broken
2. a whose   b which
   c who   d which
3. a much harder than he thought it would be   b as hard as he could
   c much sunnier than this one   d even fatter than Jodie's

27 Clauses 2 p34

1. a because we wanted to live by the sea.
   b provided we were home by five o'clock.
   c after we'd finished our homework.
   d as soon as we'd had breakfast.
2. a after the game was over   b just as the train arrived
   c before you eat your dinner
3. a provided   b when   c but   d because

28 Apostrophes p35

1. a It's no use, I can't sleep.
   b You should've said. I could've helped.
   c They mustn't go yet. I haven't said goodbye.
   d "That's strange! Where's Tom?"
   e Who's got a torch? It's dark in here!
2. a Sophie's book.   b The fox's tail.
   c The trainers' laces.   d Ranjit and Stuart's project.
3. couldn't / Mum's / 3 o'clock / Grandpa's / Mum's / could've / We'd / Jones' / Grandpa's / sister's

29 Dialogue p36

1. a "Look!" the boy shouted. "Look up there!"
   b "Come here, Tom," demanded Dad, "and sort your room out!"
   c "Stop!" bellowed the policeman. "Stop at once!"
   d "Where on earth did I put my keys?" muttered Mum.
2. "Mum?" shouted Azram.
   "Yes," replied Mum. "What's the matter?"
   "I can't find my school bag. I have looked in my bedroom, in your room and in Raj's room but it doesn't seem to be here. Can you see it downstairs anywhere?"
   "I haven't noticed it down here," said Mum, "but I'll have a look for you."
   "Thanks, Mum. You're the best!" said Azram.

30 Commas p37

1. a Mr Reeves handed out pens, rulers, individual whiteboards and cloths to the class.
   b Despite the fact that she had a cold, she was prepared to sing in the choir.
   c Meanwhile, back stage, tension was mounting.
   d Hans Christian Anderson, the Danish writer, is famous for his fairy tales.
   e I wanted a bike, a computer game, some books and a pair of shoes for my birthday.
   f William I, known as William the Conqueror, invaded England in 1066.
2. a Outside, the playground was empty.
   b I want you to go with Mary, Jamil.
   c Michael and James, the Petersen twins, are rowing.
   d For afternoon tea, cakes and rolls were served.
3. a My uncle Ted is a teacher. / Ted is one of my uncles.
   b My uncle, Ted, is a teacher. / My only uncle, Ted, is a teacher.
   c Animals which are dangerous are to be avoided./ Some animals are dangerous.
   d Animals, which are dangerous, are to be avoided. / All animals are dangerous.

31 Nonsense poetry p38

1. He was lonely: very few people come by.
2. Possible answers include:
   The hat is made of beaver skin. It is 102 feet wide. It is decorated with ribbons and bibbons and bells, buttons, loops and lace.
3. The Quangle Wangle, the Fimble Fowl, the Golden Grouse, the Pobble, the Dong, the Blue Babboon, the Orient Calf, the Attery squash, the Bisky Bat.
4. It was a 'spot so charmingly airy'.
5. bells and buttons / loops and lace / Jam and Jelly / Fimble Fowl / Bumble-Bee / Golden Grouse / Blue Babboon / Bisky Bat / Mulberry moon
6. ribbons and bibbons
7. happy and bouncy
8. Answers might include: the enjoyment of the nonsense words, the rhythm and rhyme of the poem, the strangeness of the creatures, the vividness of the descriptions.

32 Balanced arguments p40

1. The first fact states that most children in the UK wear uniform.
2. as / and that / On the other hand / and because / While / However / while
3. Some people believe / Considerable debate has taken place / Supporters of school uniform believe / They state / many people would argue
4. normal clothes **might** be / clothing **could** take / people **would** argue / and **would** support / asking **if** anyone / pupils **might** dislike / schools **should** have / now it **might**
5. School uniform helps provide a positive way of reducing discipline problems; it increases school safety; school uniform does not distract a pupil's attention away from their studies.
6. Children are more interested in labels than in school work.
7. Normal clothes do not distract a pupil's attention from their studies.
8. The argument suggests those against school uniform could provide proof by asking children if they have ever been distracted from work by someone's shirt being too bright.
9. Yes, the writer includes a qualified personal opinion in the last sentence, introducing his/her view by stating: 'it is this writer's view that'.

10 Possible answers include:
    Yes, because it gives arguments for and against wearing school uniform before drawing a conclusion on the evidence presented.

How am I doing? p42
1 **a** generally **b** generous **c** marriage **d** handkerchief **e** memorable
2 Possible answers include:
   a automobile /autograph / autobiography /automatic
   b television / telephone / telescope   **c** submarine / submerge / subject
3 **a** microphone **b** understand **c** audience
4 **a** around **b** half **c** small
5 **a** A bad workman always blames his tools. **b** A fool and his money are soon parted.
   c A penny saved is a penny gained. **d** Everything must have a beginning.
   e More haste less speed.
6 **a** The window was broken by Mike. **b** The sun was shining.
   c The crayons were placed on the table by Ranjna.
7 **a** No dogs allowed. **b** No parking. **c** Don't do that!
8 **a** "Before you sit down, can you pass me my cup of tea?"
   b He went to the concert, even though he had a headache.
   c While he was in Rome, he went to see an opera.
9 **a** The cheerful, friendly waiter brought four bowls of delicious rosy red raspberries.
   b The long-limbed giraffe stood next to his small, stumpy baby by the narrow stream.
   c He put the heavy red book and bright blue folder on the large maple coffee table.
10 **a** If / would **b** could / if **c** could / provided that
11 **a** isn't / dad's / mum's **b** Sally's / Jess's **c** can't / Raj's / won't / We'll
12 **a** "Let's go to the park," Steve called over the fence to Roger. "Ted's there already."
   b "Gran, can we make some angel cakes" asked Bella, "for Mum's birthday?"
   c "Look at this mess!" bellowed Mr Jones. "Did you really need to do all this?"

33 Spelling rules 1 p44
1 **a** Drop the e and add the suffix.
   b riper **c** nicer **d** ruder **e** closer **f** whiter
2 **a** Double the last letter then add the suffix.
   b planning **c** letting **d** knitting **e** shopping **f** drumming
3 **a** Change the y to i and then add the suffix.
   b chilliest **c** tiniest **d** easiest **e** happiest **f** funniest
4 **a** careful / careless / carefully **b** pitiful / pitiless / pitifully
   c painful / painless / painfully

34 Spelling rules 2 p45
1 **a** Change the y to an i and add es.
   b berries **c** families **d** puppies **e** sties **f** parties
2 **a** Change the f to v and add es.
   b knives **c** loaves **d** thieves **e** lives **f** shelves
3 **a** mischief **b** ✓ **c** neighbour **d** friend **e** height
   f ceiling **g** ✓ **h** ✓ **i** ✓

35 Spelling rules 3 p46
1 **a** ceiling **b** field **c** piece **d** relief
2 **a** eight **b** weight **c** skein **d** reins
3 **a** doubt **b** knight **c** lamb **d** whistle **e** island

36 Irregular words p47
1 **a** choir **b** character **c** scheme **d** echo
2 **a** science **b** antique **c** brochure **d** machine
3 **a** obey **b** grey **c** cheque **d** neighbour
4 Answers will vary.

37 Similes p48
1 **a** mule **b** arrow **c** drowned **d** whether **e** ABC
2 as quick as a flash / as happy as larks / like building blocks / as brown as berries / as pleased as punch
3 Answers will vary
4 Answers will vary

38 Metaphors p49
1 **a** is a tip **b** were pools of chocolate **c** traffic was murder
   d a heart of stone **e** is a small wilderness
2 **a** green carpet **b** red-handed **c** ball of flames **d** little monkey **e** thorny
3 Possible answers include:
   a The falling snow blanketed the ground.
   b The moon is a white balloon.
   c The sun is a golden ball.
   d The lightning was fireworks in the sky.

39 Modal verbs p50
1 **a** could **b** might **c** can **d** should **e** must
2 **a** may **b** couldn't **c** would **d** should
3 **a** must **b** will **c** should **d** won't

40 Instructional texts 1 p51
1 numbered points / diagrams / step-by-step details
2 **a** true **b** false **c** false **d** true **e** true **f** false **g** false
3 Possible answers include:
   • Go to the library.
   • The dictionary section is at the far end on the left.
   • There is a SAWF (a synonym, antonym and word finder) on the second shelf
   • Look up the word you need.
   • Make a note of suitable synonyms.
   • Look up synonyms of these words to check if they are more suitable.

41 Persuasive texts p52
1 opinion / powerful adjectives / powerful verbs
2 **a** false **b** true **c** true **d** false **e** false **f** true
   g true **h** true **i** false
3 b / c / e

42 Impersonal writing p53
1 a / d / e
2 Fill the kettle with water and switch it on. Cut the jelly into cubes and place it in a measuring jug. Allow the kettle to almost boil, then pour water on the jelly to the 500 ml mark. Stir until the jelly is dissolved. Leave until the jug is cool enough to touch. Pour the jelly into a dish and leave in a cool place until cold. Put in the fridge to set.

43 Synonyms and antonyms p54
1 Answers will vary.
2 **a** sad **b** slow **c** narrow **d** light
   e full **f** late **g** bad **h** dry
3 **a** old **b** interesting **c** slowly
4 **a** bright **b** Possible answers include: tight, nasty, selfish
   c idle **d** Possible answers include: shining, brilliant, glaring

44 Forms of punctuation p55
1 **a** "Shall we go for a swim?"
   b They went for a long walk.
   c "Charlie, don't do that!"
   d "Sam, come over here for a minute."
2 **a** "Ouch, I have just pricked my thumb."
   b "Why can't I have a drink?"
   c "Mum, I'm ever so thirsty," said little Fred.
   d In her basket were eggs, cheese, bread and butter.
3 Walt Disney's most well-known characters are Mickey Mouse, Minnie Mouse, Donald Duck and Goofy.

45 Bullet points p56
1 • Long jump
   • High jump
   • A relay race
2 Answers should include these points:
   • Turn right out of the school gate
   • At the cross roads turn left
   • Acorn Avenue is down on the right
   • My house is number 28.
3 • Place your dog in the bath and turn on the shower.
   • Rub shampoo into its fur until a thick cream is formed.
   • Wash off the shampoo very carefully, especially around the dog's face.
   • Turn off the shower and dry your dog thoroughly with a towel.

46 Instructional texts 2 p57
1 Answers will vary.
2 Answers will vary, but ensure the language is formal: You are invited to a party on…
3 The instructions should be written in an impersonal style, using imperatives and should follow a clear, logical and sequential order.
4 Answers will vary.

47 Comparing poems p58
1 A is a rhyming poem, B is blank verse.
2 The sea.
3 **a** A / strength **b** B / weakness **c** B / strength **d** A / weakness
4 Possible answers include:
   Poem A evokes a feeling of longing from the reader – it makes the reader want to run away to sea. It creates a sense of freedom.
   Poem B evokes a warm, happy feeling and takes the reader back to their own childhood memories – it is likely that everyone has experienced running into the sea when they were younger.
5 Possible answers include:
   Poem A includes many descriptive phrases which create vivid pictures of what it is like to sail on the open sea. The rhythm of the poem is bouncy, and the idea that it gives of freedom and excitement is very appealing.
   Poem B takes the reader back to their own memories of holidays playing in the sea. It describes a common experience of which most readers will have knowledge and makes it easy for the reader to picture what the poet is remembering. The familiar language of the poem will appeal to most readers.
6 Answers will vary.

48 Skimming and scanning p60
1 The life and work of Michael Foreman.
2 **a** No – the background section looks very brief
   b No – the background section looks very brief
   c Yes – the heading of the second section is 'Career'
3 The heading of the third is 'Inspirational sources' and sounds more interesting than 'Background' or 'Career'.
4 He is an author and one of the world's leading illustrators of children's books.
5 Born in Pakefield, Suffolk – 1938.
6 He has designed TV commericals and Christmas stamps.
7 Over 100 books
8 He has written 30 books.
9 He has won many prizes – the Kate Greenaway Award, for example.
10 He has gained inspiration from his trips abroad – to places such as China, Japan and the Himalayas – and from the myths and legends of Cornwall.

How am I doing? p62
1 If a root ends in y, change the y to i and then add the suffix.
2 i before e except after c.
3 Possible answers include:
   a **N**ever **E**at **C**hocolate **E**clairs **S**ince **S**ome **A**re **R**ather **Y**ucky / **O**ne collar and **t**wo sleeves.
   b **B**abies **e**at **c**ustard **a**nd **u**ncles **s**uck **e**ggs.
4 **a** miniphoto / a small photograph **b** aerophobia / fear of air
   c octology / study of the number 8 **d** autogram / a record of oneself
5 **a** fish **b** bat **c** hills **d** log
6 **a** snowed under **b** glistening jewel **c** monster
7 **a** true **b** false **c** false
8 **a** false **b** true
9 **a** ✓ **b** ✗
10 **a** ✗ **b** ✓
11 **a** The house was sold for double the amount that was paid for it.
   b The project was completed two days before the deadline.
12 Before you start, ensure there is an adult with you. The aim is to find out if it takes twice as long to boil twice as much water.
   1 First, pour enough water for 2 cups into a kettle.
   2 Switch the kettle on and start the stopwatch.
   3 As soon as the kettle boils, stop the watch and note the time.
   4 Fill the kettle with enough water for 4 cups.
   5 Switch the kettle on again and start the stopwatch.
   6 Note down the time taken.
   7 Compare with the result for 2 cups and draw your conclusion.

Clauses 1

Grammar | **Lesson 26**

> Sentences are made up of clauses, sometimes one but often two or more.
>
> **Relative clauses** are joined to the main clauses with **relative** pronouns: **who, which, where, why, whose, that.**
>
> **Comparative clauses**, as the name suggests, **compare** one part of a sentence with another using words like **better, more, as, than, like, worse,**

1. **Underline the relative clauses in these sentences.**

    a The school which he went to was a mile away.

    b The letter that you wrote arrived this morning.

    c The team for whom I play has a match on Saturday.

    d My dad whose thumb is broken finds it difficult to drive.

2. **Put the relative pronouns into these sentences.**

    which   whose   which   who

    a He stayed with Tony _____ house was much warmer.

    b She went to Emily's house _____ was next door.

    c Jenny, _____ was in her costume, looked great.

    d The shirt, _____ was blue, matched his jeans.

3. **Underline the comparative clauses in these sentences.**

    a The test was hard, much harder than he thought it would be.

    b He worked as hard as he could to finish the project.

    c Last weekend was sunny, much sunnier than this one.

    d Kelly's cat is fat, even fatter than Jodie's.

0			12
Tough		OK	Got it!

Total /12

Lesson 27 Grammar

Clauses 2

> Adverbial clauses tell us about **time, comparison, reason, purpose, contrast** and **condition**.
>
> They are usually linked to the main clause with a conjunctions such as **after, when, before, in case, although, provided, because, just, but**.
>
>   I took my raincoat **in case** it rained.
>
> The main clause makes a statement: **I took my raincoat**. The adverbial clause tells the result: **in case it rained**.

1. **Underline the adverbial clauses in these sentences.**

   a We moved to Bexhill because we wanted to live by the sea.

   b Mum said we could go to the park provided we were home by five o'clock.

   c Dad said that we could watch could television after we'd finished our homework.

   d We went to Tommy's house as soon as we'd had breakfast.

2. **Write the adverbial clauses in these sentences.**

   a We left the grounds after the game was over.

   When did they leave? _____

   b They reached the station just as the train arrived.

   When did they reach the station? _____

   c "You must wash your hands before you eat your dinner."

   When must you wash your hands? _____

3. **Use a different link word for these adverbial clauses.**

   a You can borrow my car _____ you give it back to me.

   b She went inside _____ it got dark.

   c He tried to build a castle _____ it kept tumbling down.

   d She ran outside _____ the rain stopped.

Apostrophes

Punctuation — Lesson 28

> **Apostrophes** have two main uses.
>
> - They **replace missing letters** in **contractions**.
>
>   I **ha**d = I'd.
>
> - They show **possession**.
>
>   The bag belonging to the **girl**.   The girl**'s** bag.
>
>   The books belonging to the **children**.   The children**'s** books.
>
>   The bags belonging to the **girls**.   The girls**'** bags.

1. Rewrite these sentences using apostrophes where possible.

    a It is no use, I cannot sleep. _____

    b You should have said. I could have helped. _____

    c They must not go yet. I have not said goodbye. _____

    d "That is strange! Where is Tom?" _____

    e Who has got a torch? It is dark in here! _____

2. Rewrite these phrases, using an apostrophe to show possession.

    a The book belonging to Sophie. _____

    b The tail belonging to the fox. _____

    c The laces of the trainers. _____

    d The project belonging to Ranjit and Stuart. _____

3. Write in all the missing apostrophes in this passage.   *(10 marks)*

    We couldnt wait to get into Mums car. We left at 3 o clock and set off for Grandpas house. Dad agreed with Mums suggestion to drive through the villages, although we couldve taken the motorway. Wed have a more interesting journey that way. We passed Mr Jones sheep in the field. It was quite a long journey to Grandpas so I read some of my sisters book.

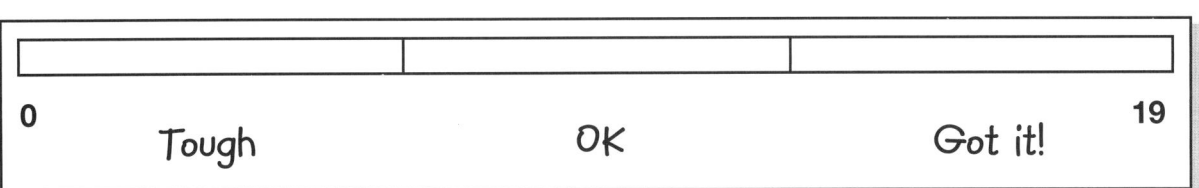

Lesson 29 Punctuation

Dialogue

> **Speech marks** indicate **direct speech** in text. When a sentence of speech is **interrupted** by narrative, **commas** are used to show the interruption and the speech continues with a **small letter**. For example:
> "If you want my opinion," said Julie, "that colour doesn't suit you at all!"
> If a **new** sentence starts after the interruption, it begins with a capital letter.
> "Where is Sanjay?" asked Keri. "He was here a minute ago!"

1. Rewrite these sentences and put in the missing punctuation.

   a Look the boy shouted Look up there

   b Come here Tom demanded Dad and sort your room out

   c Stop bellowed the policeman Stop at once

   d Where on earth did I put my keys muttered Mum

2. Rewrite this passage correctly, adding in all the missing punctuation and capital letters. *(6 marks)*

   mum shouted azram yes replied mum whats the matter i cant find my school bag i have looked in my bedroom in your room and in rajs room but it doesnt seem to be here can you see it downstairs anywhere i havent noticed it down here said mum but ill have a look for you thanks mum youre the best said azram

   QUICK TIP! Start a new line when a different character speaks.

0 Tough   OK   Got it! 10

Total /10

Commas

Punctuation — Lesson 30

> **Single commas** are used to:
> - separate items in a **list**.   Apples, pears, bananas and grapes.
> - separate **clauses** and **comments**.   Although it was cold, he wore a T-shirt.
> - **clarify** meaning in **ambiguous** phrases.   Call me Sam. / Call me, Sam.
>
> **Pairs of commas** are used to:
> - **embed** a **subordinate clause** in a main clause.
>   He said, although it wasn't true, that he'd flown to the moon.
> - separate **extra** (non-essential) **information** from the rest of a sentence.
>   My dad, who can do anything, told me that he could lift up an elephant.

1. **Add the missing commas to these sentences.**

    a Mr Reeves handed out pens rulers individual whiteboards and cloths to the class.

    b Despite the fact that she had a cold she was prepared to sing in the choir.

    c Meanwhile back stage tension was mounting.

    d Hans Christian Anderson the Danish writer is famous for his fairy tales.

    e I wanted a bike a computer game some books and a pair of shoes for my birthday.

    f William I known as William the Conqueror invaded England in 1066.

2. **Put a comma in each of these sentences to remove the ambiguities.**

    a Outside the playground was empty.

    b I want you to go with Mary Jamil.

    c Michael and James the Peterson twins are rowing.

    d For afternoon tea cakes and rolls were served.

3. **Link each sentence to its implied meaning.**

    a My uncle Ted is a teacher.   Some animals are dangerous.

    b My uncle, Ted, is a teacher.   Ted is one of my uncles.

    c Animals which are dangerous are to be avoided.   All animals are dangerous.

    d Animals, which are dangerous, are to be avoided.   My only uncle, Ted, is a teacher.

Nonsense poetry

Lesson 31 Comprehension

> **Nonsense poetry** is poetry that is not serious. It tends to include:
> - made up words
> - a story that does not make proper sense
> - a strong use of rhyme and alliteration.
>
> The most famous writer of nonsense poetry is Edward Lear.

Read this poem by Edward Lear at least twice, then answer the questions.

The Quangle Wangle's Hat

I

On the top of the Crumpetty Tree
The Quangle Wangle sat,
But his face you could not see,
On account of his Beaver Hat.
For his hat was a hundred and two feet wide,
With ribbons and bibbons on every side
And bells, and buttons, and loops, and lace,
So that nobody ever could see the face
Of the Quangle Wangle Quee.

II

The Quangle Wangle said
To himself on the Crumpetty Tree, —
'Jam; and jelly; and bread;
'Are the best food for me!
'But the longer I live on this Crumpetty Tree
'The plainer that ever it seems to me
'That very few people come this way
'And that life on the whole is far from gay!'
Said the Quangle Wangle Quee.

III

But there came to the Crumpetty Tree,
Mr. and Mrs. Canary;
And they said, — 'Did you ever see
'Any spot so charmingly airy?
'May we build a nest on your lovely Hat?
Mr. Quangle Wangle, grant us that!
'O please let us come and build a nest
'Of whatever material suits you best,
'Mr. Quangle Wangle Quee!'

IV

And besides, to the Crumpetty Tree
Came the Stork, the Duck, and the Owl;
The Snail, and the Bumble-Bee,
The Frog, and the Fimble Fowl;
(The Fimble Fowl, with a Corkscrew leg;)
And all of them said, — We humbly beg,
'We may build our homes on your lovely Hat, —
'Mr. Quangle Wangle, grant us that!
'Mr. Quangle Wangle Quee!'

V

And the Golden Grouse came there,
And the Pobble who has no toes, —
And the small Olympian bear, —
And the Dong with a luminous nose.
And the Blue Babboon, who played the flute, —
And the Orient Calf from the Land of Tute, —
And the Attery Squash, and the Bisky Bat, —
All came and built on the lovely Hat
Of the Quangle Wangle Quee.

VI

And the Quangle Wangle said
To himself on the Crumpetty Tree, —
'When all these creatures move
'What a wonderful noise there'll be!'
And at night by the light of the Mulberry moon
They danced to the flute of the Blue Babboon,
On the broad green leaves of the Crumpetty Tree,
And all were as happy as happy could be,
With the Quangle Wangle Quee.

1. Why was the Quangle Wangle Quee not happy?

   _____

2. What do we know about the hat? (3 marks)

   _____

3. Make a list of all the made-up animals in the poem.

   _____

4. What attracted the creatures to the tree?

   _____

5. Write down four pairs of words that alliterate in the poem. (4 marks)

   _____

6. Find an internal rhyme in the first verse of the poem.

   _____

7. Which of these phrases best describes the mood and rhythm of the poem? Circle one answer.

   sad and slow   exciting and rapid

   happy and bouncy   frightening and heavy

> **QUICK TIP!**
> Sometimes in poetry you get words that rhyme within a line: 'He had a fish on a dish'. These are called **internal rhymes**.

8. The poem has no real story yet it is enjoyable to read. Can you suggest why?

   _____

   _____

0	Tough	OK	Got it! 13

Total /13

39

Lesson 32 Comprehension

Balanced arguments

An argument is a **discussion** or **debate** in which people say what they think, either in **support** of or **against** a topic. Discussion texts aim to present a **balanced** view of all points surrounding a subject. An effective, balanced written argument might contain:

- a title in the form of a **question**
- **facts** or statistics and the **scope** of the argument in the introduction
- statements **for** and **against** the argument
- a **summary** at the end
- **debating terms** such as: some people believe … / it is undeniable that …
- use of **conditionals** where appropriate: would / could / should / might
- a logical structure, using **connectives**: furthermore / however / as a result.

Read this article, and then answer the questions.

> **Should children be made to wear school uniform?**
> Most pupils in the UK wear a school uniform. It is a tradition dating back to Tudor times. Some people believe that school uniform helps provide a positive way of reducing discipline problems and increasing school safety. Considerable debate has taken place over many years as to whether school uniform has now had its day.
>
> Supporters of school uniform believe that normal clothes might be distracting to a pupil's studies and that the clothing could take attention away from the purpose of school. They state that pupils are more interested in clothing labels than work. On the other hand, many people would argue that pupils do not wear clothes in order to distract other pupils and would support this by asking if anyone has complained of being unable to do their work because someone's shirt was too bright.
>
> While there are clearly many reasons why pupils might dislike school uniform, there are also many reasons why schools should have one. However, it is this writer's view that now it might be time to provide uniforms that, while being hard-wearing and smart, do appeal more to those who have to wear them.

1. What is the first fact introduced by the article?

   _____

2. Circle the connectives used in the article.   (4 marks, ½ mark each)

3. Which debating terms are included in the article? _____

   _____

4. Underline the conditional terms the author uses in the article.   (4 marks)

5. What arguments are put forward supporting school uniform? _____

   _____

6. What evidence is given to support this view? _____

   _____

7. What arguments are put forward against wearing school uniform? _____

   _____

8. What evidence is given to support this view? _____

   _____

9. Does the writer include any personal opinions? Explain your answer.

   _____

   _____

10. Do you think this article presents a balanced argument? Why?

    _____

    _____

0			16	Total
Tough	OK		Got it!	/16

41

How am I doing?

1. **Rewrite these words correctly, putting in the missing unstressed letters.**

   a genrally _____   b genrous _____   c marrige _____

   d hankerchief _____   e memrable _____

2. **Write two words that begin with each prefix.**

   a auto   _____   _____

   b tele   _____   _____

   c sub   _____   _____

3. **Complete each sentence with a word that begins with the prefix in brackets.**

   a I used a _____ when I sang at the karaoke night. (micro)

   b They spoke in another language which she couldn't _____. (under)

   c We sat in the front row of the _____ and watched the show. (audi)

4. **What do these Latin and Greek prefixes mean?**

   a circum   _____

   b semi   _____

   c micro   _____

5. **Match the first part of these proverbs with the second part.**

   a A bad workman   is a penny gained.

   b A fool and his money   less speed.

   c A penny saved   always blames his tools.

   d Everything must have   are soon parted.

   e More haste   a beginning.

6. **Change these sentences from active to passive.**

   a Mike broke the window. _____

   b The sun shone. _____

   c Ranjna placed the crayons on the table. _____

7. **Rewrite these phrases using imperatives.**

    a Your dogs are not allowed in this hotel. _____

    b Parking is not permitted in this area. _____

    c Please do not do that. _____

8. **Underline the subordinate clauses in these sentences.**

    a "Before you sit down, can you pass me my cup of tea?"

    b He went to the concert, even though he had a headache.

    c While he was in Rome, he went to see an opera.

9. **Cross out all the non-essential words, without changing the basic meaning.**

    a The cheerful, friendly waiter brought four bowls of delicious rosy red raspberries.

    b The long-limbed giraffe stood next to his small, stumpy baby by the narrow stream.

    c He put the heavy red book and bright blue folder on the large maple coffee table.

10. **Circle the conditional terms in these sentences.**

    a If I won the competition, then I would organise a large party to celebrate.

    b You could become unhealthy if you eat too much junk food.

    c He could go home early provided that he finished his work first.

11. **Write in all the missing apostrophes in these sentences.**

    a "Danny, isnt that your dads new car? Or is it your mums?"

    b The book was Sallys but as she had read it she swapped it for Jesss magazine.

    c We cant go to the park as Rajs van wont start. Well have to stay in instead.

12. **Write all the missing punctuation into these sentences.**

    a Lets go to the park Steve called over the fence to Roger Teds there already

    b Gran, can we make some angel cakes asked Bella for Mums birthday

    c Look at this mess bellowed Mr Jones Did you really need to do all this

Total

/40

Lesson 33 | Spelling

Spelling rules 1

> The spelling of some root words **does not** change if a suffix is added:
> **wish**　　　　　　**wish**ed
> But the spelling of some other root words **does** have to be changed:
> **hop**　　　　　　**hop**ped
> There are **three** general rules for words whose spelling changes when a suffix is added.

1. What is the rule for words ending in e if the suffix begins with a vowel?

   a _____

   　ripe　　nice　　rude　　close　　white

   Use the rule to add the suffix **er** to the words above.

   b _____　c _____　d _____　e _____　f _____

2. What is the rule for words with a short vowel sound when adding a suffix?

   a _____

   　plan　　let　　knit　　shop　　drum

   Use the rule to add the suffix **ing** to the words above.

   b _____　c _____　d _____　e _____　f _____

3. What is the rule for words ending in y?

   a _____

   　chilly　　tiny　　easy　　happy　　funny

   Use the rule to add the suffix **est** to the words above.

   b _____　c _____　d _____　e _____　f _____

4. Add the suffixes ful, less and fully to these words.

   a care　　_____　　_____　　_____

   b pity　　_____　　_____　　_____

   c pain　　_____　　_____　　_____

Spelling rules 2

Spelling | Lesson 34

> Many singular nouns are made into plurals by just adding **s** or **es**:
>
> **book** / **book**s   **brush** / **brush**es
>
> But the spelling of some nouns must be **changed** before they are made plural:
>
> **story** / **stor**ies   **wife** / **wives**
>
> Many words have the common letter strings **ie** or **ei**. This rhyme explains which one to use:
>
> **Use i before e, except after c. When a or i is the sound, it's the other way round.**

1. What is the rule for pluralising words ending in a consonant and y?

   a _____

   berry   family   puppy   sty   party

   Use the rule to pluralise the words above.

   b _____ c _____ d _____ e _____ f _____

2. What is the rule for pluralising words ending in f or fe?

   a _____

   knife   loaf   thief   life   shelf

   Use the rule to pluralise the words above.

   b _____ c _____ d _____ e _____ f _____

3. **Use the i before e rule to check the spelling of these words. Tick the correct spellings and write the incorrect spellings correctly.**

   a mischeif _____   b deceive _____   c nieghbour _____

   d freind _____   e hieght _____   f cieling _____

   g kaliedoscope _____   h interview _____   i fierce _____

Tough   OK   Got it!   0 — 21

Total /21

Lesson 35 | Spelling

Spelling rules 3

> Spelling words with **ei** or **ie** in them can be tricky.
> When the sound is **ee** write **ie**. When it comes after letter c write ei.
>
> **believe**   **receive**
>
> There are exceptions to the rule so if you are not sure use a dictionary.
>
> There are also some very tricky words – they have silent letters in them, words like
>
> **thistle** and **solemn**.

1. Write the correct ei or ie words in these sentences.

   a A large lamp hung from the _____ (ceiling/cieling)

   b The _____ was full of horses. (feild/field)

   c A large _____ of chocolate cake was on her plate. (piece/peice)

   d It was a big _____ to get in out of the rain. (relief/releif)

2. Choose the correct word for these sentences.

   eight   reins   weight   skein

   a Tomorrow she would be _____ years old.

   b The _____ of her suitcase was too heavy for her to carry.

   c Granny held the _____ of wool in her hands.

   d She held on tightly to the horse's _____.

3. Write the correctly spelt words in these sentences.

   a She did not _____ his word. (dout/doubt)

   b He was a _____ in shining armour. (knight/night)

   c They had roast _____ for dinner. (lam/lamb)

   d The referee blew his _____ (whisle/whistle)

   e They rowed across the river to a small _____ (iland/island)

Irregular words

Spelling | Lesson 36

> Some groups of letters have entirely different pronunciations from what you would expect. Here are some of them.
>
> **sch** is pronounced as **sk** in words like school
> **ch** can be pronounced as **k** as in chemist or **sh** in chef
> **sc** is pronounced as **s** in words like scene
> **que** is pronounced as as **guh** in league or **k** as in unique
> **ey** is pronounced as as **ay** in **they**.

1. **Use these words to complete these sentences.**

    scheme   choir   character   echo

    a She sang in the school _____.

    b He was the main _____ in the school play.

    c Dad had to prepare a new _____ of work for Year 7.

    d She could hear her voice _____ in the empty corridor.

2. **Choose the correct spelling for the missing words.**

    a Her favourite subject was _____. (sience/science)

    b The piece of furniture was an _____. (antick/antique)

    c We designed a new _____ for Dad's business. (brochure/broshure)

    d It was fun having a go on Mum's sewing _____. (mashine/machine)

3. **Correct the misspelt words in these sentences.**

    a The Head said that we must _____ the school rules. (obay/obey)

    b There was a _____ squirrel up in the oak tree. (grey/gray)

    c Dad decided to pay by _____. (chek/cheque)

    d Tim is my next door _____. (naybour/neighbour)

0			12
Tough	OK	Got it!	

Total 12

Lesson 37 | Spelling

Similes

> Similes (pronounced sim-ill-lees) create a picture in the reader's mind by **comparing** one thing with another, usually to **exaggerate**:
>
> The giant was **as big as a house**.   The horse was **as white as snow**.
>
> The avalanche swept down the mountain **like an express train**.

1. **Use the correct spelling of these words to complete the similes.**

    whether/weather   mool/mule   arrow/arow   ACB/ABC   drained/drowned

    a Gavin could be as stubborn as a _____ .

    b The flight of the ball was as swift as an _____ .

    c Stuart came in from the rain looking like a _____ rat.

    d Lorna didn't know _____ to go swimming or not.

    e Once he had read the instructions it was as simple as _____ .

2. **Underline the similes in this piece of writing.**

    We were packed as quick as a flash and as happy as larks to be leaving this place. The luggage was stacked like building blocks in the foyer. We were as brown as berries from the sun but were as pleased as punch to be moving on.

3. **Complete the similes using different words from the usual ones given in brackets.**

    a as quiet as _____ (a mouse)   **b** as tough as _____ (nails)

    c as bright as _____ (a button)   **d** as strong as _____ (an ox)

    e run like _____ (the wind)   **f** as thick as _____ (thieves)

4. **Use your own endings to complete these similes.**

    a It was as cheap as _____ .   **b** The plant was as dead as _____ .

    c It was as smooth as _____ .   **d** His brain was as sharp as _____ .

    e Her feet were as warm as _____ . **f** He was as sly as a _____ .

0			18	Total
Tough	OK	Got it!		/18

Metaphors

Spelling — Lesson 38

> A **metaphor** describes something as if it is something else, suggesting **similarities** but not comparing things in the way that similes do. Metaphors help to create a vivid picture for the reader and make narrative and poetry much more interesting:
>
> His daughter was the **apple** of his eye.

1. Underline the metaphors in these sentences.

    a "Your bedroom is a tip!" shouted Mum.

    b Her dog's eyes were pools of chocolate.

    c "Sorry I'm late, the traffic was murder!"

    d He had a heart of stone.

    e The garden is a small wilderness.

2. Complete each metaphor with the appropriate word or phrase below.

    red-handed   green carpet   thorny   little monkey   ball of flames

    a The grass was a _____ .

    b He was caught _____ .

    c Soon after the fire started the house was a _____ .

    d Her son was a _____ on Saturday!

    e It was a _____ question.

3. Make up your own metaphors to complete these sentences.

    a The falling snow _____

    b The moon is _____

    c The sun is _____

    d The lightning was _____

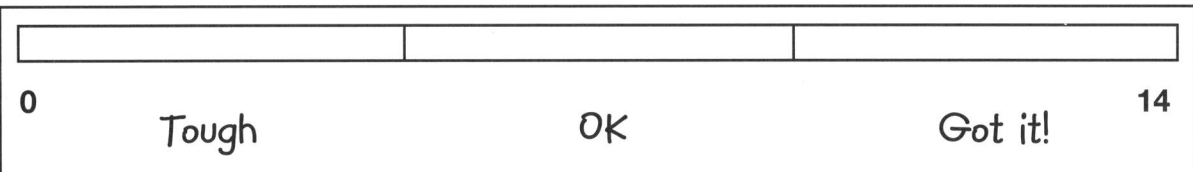

Total /14

Lesson 39 Grammar

Modal verbs

> Modal verbs are 'helping' verbs. They help the main verb express a range of meanings.
> I **can** go swimming   or   I **could** go swimming.

1. **Modal verbs express possibility.**

    can   could   might   should   must

    a _____ you pick up my paper for me?

    b This book _____ come in useful.

    c We _____ go to Grandad's tomorrow.

    d Jack _____ be here by five o'clock.

    e I _____ finish my homework.

2. **Modal verbs can form negatives and ask questions.**

    would   couldn't   may   should

    a We _____ go to the park later.

    b I _____ stop laughing at James.

    c Dad, _____ you give me a lift to Fred's house?

    d We _____ be home by seven o'clock.

3. **They can be used to express what possibly or certainly might happen.**

    won't   must   should   will

    a You _____ tell me exactly what happened.

    b That _____ be Charlie ringing the doorbell.

    c We _____ get to the station on time.

    d Sorry Tom, we _____ be going to the pictures tonight.

0			13	Total
Tough	OK	Got it!		/13

Instructional texts 1

Grammar | **Lesson 40**

> Instructions and directions are best written in a clear, compact style. They should use just enough words to keep them clear and understandable, while providing all the essential information.

1. **Circle the features that are most useful in an instructional text.**

   numbered points   chapters   diagrams   conclusion   step-by-step details

2. **Decide whether these statements about instructional texts are true or false.**

   a Instructional texts should be written in clear, precise language. _____

   b Any adverbs in instructional texts should be chosen for their vividness, not clarity. _____

   c Instructional texts are often written in the first person singular. _____

   d Instructional texts usually start by stating the aim of the instructions. _____

   e Information in instructional texts is often organised using bullet points. _____

   f Numbered lists are never used in instructional texts. _____

   g A fictional story is an example of an instructional text. _____

3. **Read these instructions for finding synonyms in a book in the library then rewrite them more clearly and concisely, removing any unnecessary information. Think carefully about the way in which instructions are usually presented.**   *(8 marks)*

   Go to the library upstairs. You'll like it up there because there are so many books! The section for dictionaries is at the far end on your left. On the second shelf you will find a SAWF (a synonym, antonym and word finder) – it seems a very strange name for a book. Look up the word you need. Make a note of suitable synonyms. Then look up some of the synonyms for those words too because they might be more suitable.

   _____

   _____

   _____

   _____

0   Tough   OK   Got it!   16   Total /16

Lesson 41 | Grammar

Persuasive texts

> **Persuasive writing** is written with the aim of changing other people's views – not always a very easy task!
>
> Effective persuasive writing is often a combination of appeals to our **emotions** (feelings and reactions) and our **head** (logic and argument).

1. **Circle the features you would expect to find in a persuasive text.**

    opinion   powerful adjectives   chapters   powerful verbs   table of contents

2. **Decide whether these statements about persuasive texts are true or false.**

    a Persuasive texts offer objective points of view. _____

    b Persuasive texts often include phrases of exaggeration. _____

    c The key issue of a persuasive text is usually detailed in the opening phrases. _____

    d Rhetorical questions are not used in persuasive writing. _____

    e Persuasive texts only present facts about an issue or topic. _____

    f Persuasive texts often disguise opinion as fact. _____

    g Persuasive texts aim to provoke an emotional response from the reader. _____

    h Persuasive texts often repeat key facts and arguments. _____

    i Persuasive texts always present a complete and fully supported argument. _____

3. **Tick these sentences if you think they come from persuasive texts.**

    a In Cambridge there are 42 zebra crossings to make the city safer for pedestrians. ___

    b Washo washing powder works wonders on your clothes. Why use anything else? ___

    c Surveys show that nearly all pet owners who really care for their dogs choose Fido. ___

    d An RSPCA report stated that 80 per cent of dog owners feed their pets canned dog food. ____

    e The National Democrats – the only party that really supports hard-up pensioners. ___

0			15	Total
Tough	OK	Got it!		/15

Impersonal writing

Grammar — Lesson 42

> **Impersonal** texts
> • offer **facts** rather than personal opinions
> • are often written in the **passive** voice
> • contain **imperative verbs**
> • do not use personal pronouns such as **I** or **you**.
> 'I think you turn left at the post office' is a **personal** statement.
> 'Turn left at the post office' is an **impersonal** statement.
> Explanatory texts and non-chronological reports are examples of texts that use impersonal writing.

1. Put a tick next to the sentences that have come from impersonal texts.

a The car was driven down the road at great speed. _____

b I believe the train has arrived already. _____

c You will agree with me when you have read the rest of this article. _____

d Tennis was introduced to England during the 14th century. _____

e Bengal tigers have been living in India for many years. _____

2. Rewrite this passage as a piece of impersonal text. *(5 marks)*

I filled the kettle with water and switched it on. I cut the jelly into cubes and placed them in a measuring jug. I allowed the kettle to almost boil and then poured water onto the jelly cubes until it reached 500 ml. I stirred it until the jelly had dissolved. I then left it until I could comfortably touch the jug. I poured the jelly into a dish and left it in a cool place until it was cold then I put it in the fridge until it was set.

Fill the kettle with water _____

_____

_____

_____

_____

Lesson 43 Grammar

Synonyms and antonyms

> **Synonyms** are words that have the same or very similar meaning
>
> buy/purchase big/large quickly/speedily
>
> **Antonyms** are words with opposite meanings
>
> hot/cold large/small fat/skinny

1. Think of four words that are synonyms of the given word.

   a beautiful _____ _____ _____ _____

   b funny _____ _____ _____ _____

   c kind _____ _____ _____ _____

   d strong _____ _____ _____ _____

2. Write the antonyms for these words.

   a happy _____ b fast _____ c wide _____ d dark _____

   e empty _____ f early _____ g good _____ h wet _____

3. Write an antonyms for the underlined words.

   a His grandfather was a young man. _____

   b It was a very boring book. _____

   c They walked quickly through the park. _____

4. Write a synonym for the underlined words.

   a Meredith was a clever girl. _____

   b His cousin was a mean person. _____

   c Being lazy means you don't get much done. _____

   d The bright sun shone straight into her eyes. _____

Tough OK Got it!

Total

Forms of punctuation

Punctuation | Lesson 44

> **Punctuation** is used in all forms of writing
>
> to end a sentence   .   to create a pause   ,   to ask a question   ?
>
> for an exclamation   !   to denote speech   "Hi."

1. **Put the correct punctuation in these sentences.**

    a ___Shall we go for a swim___ ___

    b They went for a long walk ___

    c ___ Charlie ___ don't do that ___ ___

    d ___ Sam ___ come over here for a minute ___ ___

2. **Rewrite these sentences using the correct punctuation.**

    a Ouch I have just pricked my thumb

    _____

    b Why can't I have a drink

    _____

    c Mum I'm ever so thirsty said little Fred

    _____

    d In her basket were eggs cheese bread and butter

    _____

3. **Correct this sentence using commas and capital letters.**

    walt disney's most well-known characters are mickey mouse minnie mouse donald duck and goofy.

    _____

    _____

    _____

0			9
Tough	OK		Got it!

Total: /9

55

Lesson 45 Punctuation

Bullet points

> **Bullet points** are used to show information in a clear, concise and ordered way. They might include:
>
> - specific points from a text
> - important elements of information about how to do something
> - the order of events
> - items on an agenda.

1. **On Sports Day there will be a number of events** including long jump, high jump and a relay race. Use bullet points to list these events.

    Sports Day Events will include:

    - _____
    - _____
    - _____

2. Read this information and list the directions to Nick's house in bullet points.

    Patrick wanted to know how to get to Nick's house. Nick laughed and said, 'It's easy. Turn right out of the school gates and, at the crossroads, turn left. Acorn Avenue, the road where I live, is down on the right. My house is number 28.'

    - _____
    - _____
    - _____
    - _____

3. Put these instructions in the correct order.

    Place your dog in a bath and turn on the shower.
    Turn off the shower and dry your dog thoroughly with a towel.
    Wash off the shampoo very carefully especially around the dog's face.
    Rub shampoo into its fur until a thick foam has formed.

    - _____
    - _____
    - _____
    - _____

0			3
Tough		OK	Got it!

Total / 3

Instructional texts 2

Punctuation — Lesson 46

> Imagine it is your birthday and you are having a party. Decide the details of where and when it will be celebrated. Make sure that you **punctuate** your invitation, the directions and your thank you letter correctly.

1. Write down the following information:

   What date is your party? _____

   Where is it to be held? _____

   What time should your guests arrive? _____ What time should they be collected? _____

   Do they need to bring anything? _____

   What should they wear? _____

2. Write an invitation to your birthday, include all the above information.

   _____
   _____
   _____
   _____

3. Write directions for getting from school to where the party is being held.

   _____
   _____
   _____
   _____

4. Write a short 'thank you' letter to one of your friends who came to your party.

   _____
   _____
   _____
   _____

| 0 Tough | OK | Got it! 4 | Total /4 |

Lesson 47 Comprehension # Comparing poems

> There are many varieties of poems, for example: **narrative poems**, **shape poems**, **haiku**, **sonnets** and **limericks**. Each of these types of poem has different features and layouts, but they often cover similar themes. It is often interesting to compare poems by:
>
> **type** of poem **subject** **strengths** and **weaknesses** **mood** **appeal** to the reader

Read the two poems below and then answer the questions.

A

Sea Fever

I must go down to the seas again, to the lonely sea and the sky,
And all I ask is a tall ship and a star to steer her by,
And the wheel's kick and the wind's song and the white sail's shaking,
And a grey mist on the sea's face and a grey dawn breaking.

I must go down to the seas again, for the call of the running tide
Is a wild call and a clear call that may not be denied;
And all I ask is a windy day with the white clouds flying,
And the flung spray and the blown spume, and the sea-gulls crying.

I must go down to the seas again, to the vagrant gypsy life,
To the gull's way and the whale's way, where the wind's like a whetted knife;
And all I ask is a merry yarn from a laughing fellow-rover,
And quiet sleep and a sweet dream when the long trick's over.

John Masefield

B

Disevolving

As a child it was fun
To spring from the towels, aiming straight at the sea,
And have it wrestle with me,
My quick stride quenched to slow-motion,
Until – at waist high –
I could make better going
By lifting up horizontal
And flapping my limbs
Fish-wise.

Joseph Johnson

1. What is the difference between the rhymes in the two poems?

   _____

2. What is the central theme (subject) of both of these poems?

   _____

3. Decide which of the poems each of these statements refers to. Say whether each statement is a strength or a weakness.

   a The poem has a strong, clear rhythm in each verse. ___ strength / weakness

   b When read aloud, it isn't clear that it has been written as a poem. ___ strength / weakness

   c An effective description of what it is like to be in the water. ___ strength / weakness

   d It contains old English terms which can be difficult to understand. ___ strength / weakness

4. What mood or emotions do you feel each poem creates in the reader? *(2 marks)*

   Poem A _____

   _____

   Poem B _____

   _____

5. What do you think will appeal to the reader about each poem? *(2 marks)*

   Poem A _____

   _____

   Poem B _____

   _____

6. Which poem appeals to you most? Explain your answer.

   _____

   _____

   _____

0			11	Total
Tough	OK	Got it!		/11

Lesson 48 Comprehension # Skimming and scanning

> To swiftly determine what a text is about, it is useful to **skim read** the content. Skimming provides you with an **overview** and a general sense of the **main ideas** in a text. Reading elements such as a **title**, **headings**, **introduction** and **conclusion**, will quickly show if a text is relevant and should be read more closely.
>
> To quickly find a specific piece of information, it is useful to **scan** the content. Scanning allows you to focus closely on the **key details** that are important to you.
>
> You do not read every word or sentence with these techniques. You may find it useful to **underline** key terms or phrases as you skim or scan a text.

Skim read the title and headings of this passage and then answer questions 1 to 3.

Michael Foreman

He wrote and published his first book while he was still at art school. Now, Michael Foreman is one of the world's leading illustrators.

Background
Michael was born in Pakefield, Suffolk in 1938. As he grew up in wartime Britain, he read magazines, delivered newspapers and dreamed of being a footballer. At the age of 15, he went to art school and from there his natural talent was nurtured.

Career
Over his career, he has worked on magazines, book jackets and TV commercials and he has even designed Christmas stamps! However, Michael is best known for his illustrations – he has created illustrations for over 100 books for authors such as Roald Dahl and has also written and illustrated over 30 of his own stories. His talent has been frequently recognised with prizes such as the Kate Greenaway Award.

Inspirational sources
Throughout his career, Michael has travelled widely to places such as China, Japan and the Himalayas and it is from these experiences that he has gained much of his inspiration for the settings and illustrations in his work. He also takes much of his inspiration from the myths and legends of Cornwall – where he and his family have a second home – and enjoys spending much of his time by the sea. His love of the ocean is clearly shown in the range of blues used in his artwork.

1. What is the topic of this text? _____

2. From a quick skim, does the text give you the following information?

    a Who his best friend was at school. _____

    b The grades he got at school. _____

    c What types of jobs he has had. _____

3. Which section is likely to hold the most interesting information?

    _____

    Now scan the extract briefly, underline any key points and answer these questions.

4. What is Michael Foreman's job? _____

5. When and where was he born? _____

6. What else has he designed apart from book jackets and magazines?

    _____

7. How many books has he illustrated for other authors? _____

8. How many books has Michael written? _____

9. How has his talent been rewarded? _____

10. Where does Michael get his inspiration from?

    _____

    _____

    _____

			Total
0 Tough	OK	Got it! 12	/12

How am I doing?

1. Which rule was applied to these words before the suffixes were added?

   funniest   cheeriest   friendliest   prettiest   cheekiest

   _____

2. Which rule do these words follow?

   chief   receive   sieve   grief   deceit

   _____

3. Write a mnemonic you know or make one up to help you remember these spellings.

   a necessary _____

   b because _____

4. Link these invented words with their definitions.

   a miniphoto   fear of the air

   b aerophobia   a record of oneself

   c octology   study of the number 8

   d autogram   a small photograph

5. Complete these similes using one of the nouns below.

   bat   log   fish   hills

   a Ravi swam like a _____.

   b Without his glasses, he was as blind as a _____.

   c That joke was as old as the _____.

   d Dad slept like a _____.

6. Complete each metaphor with the appropriate word or phrase below.

   snowed under   monster   glistening jewel

   a Sally was _____ with work.

   b The moon is a _____.

   c Their boss is a _____!

7. **Are these statements about narrative texts true or false?**

   a Every narrative text has a narrator. _____

   b A piece of narrative text always starts with a section of dialogue. _____

   c Narrative texts are separated into scenes. _____

8. **Are these statements about instructional texts true or false?**

   a The purpose of an instructional text is to recount an event. _____

   b Instructional texts are written in the second person. _____

9. **Tick the sentence which has been taken from a persuasive text.**

   a 42 species of wildflower, three rare species of moth and eight different fungi live on Chartheath Common – it's a great place to get close to nature. _____

   b 42 species of wildflower, three rare species of moth and eight different fungi live on the Chartheath Common. _____

10. **Tick the impersonal sentence.**

    a She placed the saucer above the flame and saw the chemical reaction happen. _____

    b Press the red button on the remote control and hold for ten seconds. _____

11. **Rewrite these sentences in the passive voice.**

    a I sold the house for double the amount I paid for it.

    _____

    b We completed the project two days before the deadline.

    _____

12. **Rewrite these instructions clearly, using appropriate punctuation.**

    before you start ensure there is an adult with you the aim is to find out if it takes twice as long to boil twice as much water first pour enough water for 2 cups into a kettle switch the kettle on and start the stopwatch as soon as the kettle boils stop the watch and note the time fill the kettle with enough water for 4 cups switch the kettle on again and start the stopwatch note down the time taken compare with the result for 2 cups and draw your conclusion

    Total /27